DIAGNOSTICS OF KARMA

Lazarev S.N.

DIAGNOSTICS OF KARMA

Book 1

System of the self-regulating energy field

Table of Contents

Author's Note

Dear reader, please check your emotional state before starting to read this book. I highly recommend you refrain from reading this book if you feel resentment, irritation or any negative emotions towards others.

You're now holding not just a new book on a topic that attracts much attention, but an exposition of an original concept exploring the laws of the spiritual world, which direct the material. This is also an analysis of opportunities for entering the world of bioenergetics.

The main purpose of this book is to understand the inner and outer worlds of man, uncover and examine the laws that control them; to expose the rules of exploring bioenergetics, as personal development must start with understanding the world, comprehending its laws, perceiving oneself as a part of a united system of the universe.

Contemporary humanity has distanced itself from its spiritual origins. It is similar to a ship with a mutinous crew, a missing captain, a punctured hull and a broken down engine. Some of the crew already realizes what is going on. Calls for reconciliation and repairing the ship begin to appear. But the main problem, which remains unknown to the crew, is that the ship is heading for a reef, so even repairing the boat without changing the course cannot save the ship and its crew.

Humanity is facing a danger which is much more serious than a nuclear threat, the threat of spiritual disintegration. The most terrible losses are those we do not notice or feel, as death appears first on the energy field level, and only after does it appear to the physical body. Today the process is reaching a critical point because, what today comprises our spirit, tomorrow will become the bodies of our children and grandchildren. Thus, the more damaged our spirit is now, the more damaged the future health – spiritual and physical – of our descendants.

The information I obtained while researching the biofield structures of humanity is quite serious. The spiritual potential, accumulated by saints, psychics and founders of world religions is now almost fully depleted, and the lack of development in strategic thinking will create great problems in the future. The enormous potential of bioenergetics is directed, not at the comprehension of the surrounding world, foresight and prevention of future problems, but at solving primitive tactical daily tasks. Humanity is on the threshold beyond which lies either spiritual rebirth or death. Salvation lies in the personal spiritual quest of every person. We must realize that each of us is responsible for the fate of humanity and the life of the Universe.

Imagine this: a man who wants to learn how to drive a car is placed in a vehicle, blindfolded, given the wheel and then shown where the gas pedal is. At this point the training is finished. The numerous schools of extra sensory study, in a very short period of time and for a relatively large amount of money, will give you the same level of knowledge in the field of bioenergetics. These schools differ only in 'the model of the car' and 'the power of the engine' while one should start with learning the rules of the road and the mechanics of the automobile.

Without understanding ourselves and the surrounding world, without serious training, the effects of entering bioenergetics may be more dangerous than blindfolded driving. This book is therefore dedicated to the rules of conduct in the spiritual world.

There is one more warning. To fully disclose the topic I must provide some basic information regarding the means of entering energy field structures. I don't advise anybody, having read this book, to attempt doing the same. It is dangerous not only for the person who thoughtlessly tries to replicate my experience, but also for their relatives. Only a very limited circle of people, who have certain abilities and special training, may attempt to do this.

And lastly, many readers will find rather unexpected and new information in this book, which may be reminiscent of scenes from science fiction. But I am a researcher and – despite all the unbelievable facts and conclusions given – this is our current reality having been checked many times and proven by the results of my work.

Chapter 1

The Concept of a System
of Energy-Field Self-Regulation and
the History of its Development

When one monk – after praying for ten years to God for the gift of healing and obtaining it – came to his elder and told him about it, the wise man ordered him to go back and pray that God take the gift back and instead grant him vision of his sins.

The results of my research in the realm of bioenergetics have been obtained through 20 years of work in this area, a philosophical comprehension of the world and, also, through convincing confirmation of the main philosophic and theoretical hypotheses in practical work.

What is this book about? Humanity is now facing very serious problems, and our future depends on our ability to solve them. It is customary to believe that our main problems come from a troublesome ecology, threats of nuclear war and dozens of other external causes. In reality, the main reason for troubles is contained in man himself; to change the world we must change ourselves first.

It is much harder to change oneself than the surrounding world – we have no sources or systems explaining how to fundamentally change our thoughts, world-views and our spirituality. The ways offered by contemporary philosophers and teachers are, at best, an attempt to rehash accumulated knowledge, whereas the main point of focus should be on understanding the world and seeking ways of self-development.

To change the world and to influence it, one needs to understand it. Understanding the world is the beginning of its change. We often have distorted beliefs about the world and blindly try to conquer it, but, in fact, - we destroy it, hurting ourselves along with it. We need to realize the degree of our dependency on the world and our connection to it. We must know the laws by which the world lives and develops.

My research is focused, first of all, on understanding what man, his mentality, his subconscious and the Universe are.

It's time to leave behind the primitive materialistic concept that man begins and ends in his physical body. A human is a very complex information-energy system, composed only of a few percent body and mind. 95-98 percent of a person are information-energy layers of the subconscious, just as unknown to us as the Universe.

When dealing with issues of human health and illness prevention I first look for causes, and every time, I receive confirmation of the imperative of human spiritual development. Unfortunately, currently there is no unified system of knowledge that could help us develop our bio-energetic abilities without bringing harm to mankind. Bioenergetics has so much potential that one must be very careful, gradual, when entering its sphere, starting, first of all, with ethical development. Ethics and an understanding of the world are the highest protection, but our expertise in these areas is quite poor. Any serious action should be well prepared, as neglecting preparation may lead to degeneration and death instead of spiritual growth and positive changes. Unfortunately, these processes are present and the tendency towards degeneration already exists.

I'll try to reveal the reasons for man's pitiable physical state and show a means of improving it through correction of subtle energy fields. I will also define a competent approach towards bioenergetics and the possibilities of man's development. An understanding of the surrounding world and the highest self-discipline are preconditions for the advancement of the spirit and soul – they are now required for survival. This book contains essential information for understanding the complexity of the problems every person faces today. The point is that during the last two or three years all the energy processes on Earth have accelerated and, what is called 'karma' in Hinduism, the law of retribution, has sped up ten-fold.

All my life I've been trying to understand the world in a new way. Since childhood I felt I had innate abilities, but intuitively I didn't direct my efforts towards their development. Instead, I endeavored to understand the world as I always felt that understanding is more important than the accumulation and refining of abilities.

Many times I've heard stories about the power of a curse - that it can be passed on hereditarily through generations. Many examples can be found in literary fiction. The following story, described in the book "From the caves and jungles of Hindustan" by E. Blavadskaya touched me deeply when I read it in the 1970's. In an Indian village, Blavadskaya had a conversation with the descendant of a formerly powerful king who told her the following: during one of his trips, the king generously rewarded wise men, as it was traditional at that time, but he forgot to give a gift to one of them. This wise man was mortally offended and cursed the king. Terrified, the king fell down to his feet and started begging for forgiveness. The most interesting part of the story happens here, in my opinion. The wise man said that it was too late, the curse had already taken effect and it couldn't be stopped. As a result, king would lose his throne. However, the wise man promised to save the king's life and that of his descendants. And so it happened that the king lost his throne and his descendants were scattered all over India.

My path to bioenergetics came through casual acquaintances with magic, sorcery and different practices of folk healing. I have traveled all over the country studying them.

Every time, when analyzing new information, I strove to find the initial cause, to understand the source of a family's misfortunes, what is the reason for such phenomena as the death of a blood-line, inherited illness, and so on. It was absolutely clear to me that genes could not be the source of this information - it must be contained and passed on to descendants by an energy field. When this conviction reached a certain point I had just a "simple" thing to do – find the responsible structures in a person's energy field for retaining and transferring the information from one generation to another. I strongly believed that these structures existed and named them "stable information groupings". Since the mid-80s I persistently tried to detect them in the energy field of man.

I finally managed to achieve this goal in the beginning of 1990. Once while at the First Medical Institute, I was approached by one of the psychic healers on staff asking me to help resolve a difficult case. His patient's energy field had been torn. After treatment it would normalize for a while and then again a tear would appear.

What happened next one might call an "enlightenment". The patient's flabby, cotton-like energy field that I previously perceived as emptiness suddenly became elastic; I could feel it reacting to my intrusion. My hands detected the powerful structures penetrating the breakage in the energy field. Immediately my perception changed entirely: what I had perceived as a breakage became, for me, a stable structure causing the energy field's deformation, leading to loss of energy. I realized that I had just found that which we call "illness" in the energy field - that which determines the patient's physical state. This was a qualitative change in my understanding, as now it became possible to diagnose illnesses before their physical manifestation, that is – not only to cure them, but also prevent them.

I decided that I could put together a group of healers, teach them the method and start working on preventing many illnesses. Moreover, it wouldn't require any medication. The only thing required would be good mastery of the method. If only I had known...

I worked as a healer for a year thinking that these structures defined the condition of the physical body only. Gradually, however, I started to accumulate facts that didn't fit this concept. During the healing process I noticed that patients' characters and even destinies were noticeably changing. By analyzing these changes, I had to admit that a person's character, destiny and illnesses were somehow interrelated, but these relations were multifaceted. Particular deformations of energy field structures could manifest in various ways: they could become different diseases, mental illnesses, pathological changes in character, injuries or misfortune. Diving deeper into these facts I came to the conclusion that health, character and even a person's destiny are determined by karmic structures. All of the information about a person and his physical condition is encoded in his energy field. There is also a dialectic relationship between the energy field and physical structures and they can influence each other. Destiny and character are also encoded in energy field structures, thus if one influences them, gradually, a lot can be improved.

The more time I spent researching, the more incredible were the findings. I'll try to describe the magnitude of this method's potential based on examples of treatment of various diseases, correction of complex life situations. I will also give examples testing different events, objects of inanimate nature and other research.

At the beginning I was using traditional methods of extrasensory energy influence in my work.

One woman was in the hospital with a lung edema. She was in very bad condition, and doctors had no hope for her recovery. Her daughter approached me asking for help and I started healing from a distance. Shortly after, the patient could breathe without her oxygen mask. Doctors could not understand what was happening. Their patient was getting better and better every moment – her face gained some color, she sat in her bed and asked for something to eat, even though she had rejected food for several days.

There was another story that happened to my brother the surgeon. While operating on an elder woman who was in extremely weak condition, he cut his hand. His hand and lymph nodes became swollen and he got blood poisoning. He was in really bad shape - antibiotics didn't help. I tried to help my brother. A few minutes after I started, he felt some kind of pricking in his lymph nodes, then the swelling gradually dissolved and in an hour, his temperature dropped back to normal - he began to recover.

How did I start to heal people? I spent about ten years doing research, studying the literature on Eastern techniques and getting some knowledge about the methods of energy influence on humans. The first stimulus that led me in the direction of healing was a fact from Rasputin's biography that inspired me. A woman, who wrote a memoir about Rasputin once came to him, depressed, because her friend in Kiev was dying. When Rasputin found out about her grief he promised to save her friend. He stood in the middle of the room and turned pale in front of her eyes. His face became as white as wax. He remained in this state for two more minutes, before regaining his natural color again and announcing: 'Everything is fine, your friend will live'. A few days later a telegram came with news that the girl's life was no longer in danger.

I was reminded of Rasputin's story when my friend's daughter became ill – at first she had measles, and then complications started: meningitis and bilateral pneumonia – I decided to try influencing the situation. I really wanted to help, I had a great desire to do my duty, and if there was even negligible hope, I would use it. On Monday, about two in the afternoon, I focused and transferred my sincere wish of recovery to the girl. At the same moment, I felt almost physically that something had changed, that somehow I had made some impact. I became confident that I had managed to help. On Wednesday I met the father of the child and found out that the girl was getting better.

"When did the improvement start?" I asked him.

"Two days ago, in the afternoon at around two o'clock," was his answer.

In 1988, I was approached by the mother of a girl whose vision had started to rapidly deteriorate. The girl was undergoing medical treatment at the First Medical Institute, but despite all doctors' efforts, they couldn't find the cause of the illness and her vision continued to worsen. They could not locate the infection and antibiotic treatments did not give any result. I started to work with the girl at a distance. After the first session I noticed some improvement and offered to carry out two or three more sessions. In two weeks the girl was fully recovered and was released from the hospital with twenty-twenty vision. I didn't find the cause of this illness, but I managed to stop the process and bring her vision back.

Time passed by. The girl's vision was normal, but after a couple of months she suddenly started to feel pain in her kidneys. She was taken to the hospital with a painful attack of kidney colic where she was given antibiotics – but again there was no improvement. After a while she was released from the hospital with unsatisfying test results and aching kidneys. We had another four sessions and, again, she came to full recovery. I was delighted: medicine is powerless, no drugs could help, antibiotics gave no result and I did.

At that time I still didn't realize that all parts of the body are interrelated, I didn't know that illnesses could move from one organ to another and, moreover, I didn't know that character, destiny, spirituality and some other parameters of human beings were also part of this system.

So, the girl was healthy. More time passed. During this time my skills improved and I started to see that the human organism is a unified system, where health, destiny, character and mentality are inseparable. I saw the girl's mother and was disappointed to find out that, even though the girl was in brilliant health, she suffered a very difficult destiny. I tested the value of her destiny parameter and it was quite negative. This usually leads to great problems in life.

Thus I realized that taking care only of health issues, focusing my attention only on the body, I managed to improve one link in chain known as the "human" system, at the cost of all the others. I had healed the illness, but hadn't removed its cause and the illness was transferred to her destiny. I understood that I have to treat a person as a united system. This allowed me to see those "root" causes, which really affect all the parameters of a person.

As further testing showed, the cause of all of my patient's problems was her mother's being deeply offended at her husband during pregnancy, deforming the structure of the energy field responsible for her daughter's health and fate.

Throughout the next few years I continued to use distant healing with my patients using the energy in my hands. About five years ago I realized, for the first time, that this method was imperfect. I treated children in one family and, having noticed that their grandmother wasn't well, I offered to help her. At the beginning she refused. She told me that she had stenocardia requiring them to call an ambulance five-six times a week, but she had accepted the situation and didn't believe that there could be an improvement. Looking at her energy field I saw that her heart was healthy. We had a few sessions and her condition improved each time. On our third session, I felt with my hands a deformation of the field – there were noticeable violations of the energy field in the area of her heart. I made a few passes with my hands and the deformations would disappear, the energy field would smoothen, but after a couple days the heart condition would return.

Then I hypothesized that there must be a unknown mechanism. I needed to find out what it was. Analyzing my patient's condition I felt that it was something to do with an event in her life.

"What happened to you two years ago?" I asked.

"My sister died."

"What did you feel?"

"She was so healthy, strong – and she died, but I'm sick and still alive."

I understood the reason for her illness - colossal stress remained in her subconscious mind, which provoked her stenocardia attack. To remove it I needed to change the woman's outlook on the world, her attitude towards life and death. I explained to her that death is just a transition to another state and she shouldn't take it so tragically. We should not regret the past, as regretting it we are subconsciously trying to change it, move things that cannot be moved. This causes an uncontrollable and enormous waste of energy. To prevent this leak of energy that may lead to very serious consequences, the organism blocks it with an illness on the physical level. We had a couple of sessions of auto-suggestion training, and her attacks stopped.

Powerful stress, disagreement with something or regrets about the past especially if emotionally empowered, pile up in the subconscious mind and provoke serious illnesses, as they create deformations of energy field structures. Correcting these field structures using energy can harmonize them, but not always, and most important – the very cause of the illness is not removed and can reappear any time in another place. This example confirmed that, without a clear method of diagnosis, without understanding the cause of a disease, healing blindly has no future. If I cannot explain how I am helping and what heals during sessions – it is like wandering in the darkness.

Further development of my method occurred at First Medical Institute. I was working on two issues there: healing and simultaneously trying to find ways to protect the healer from the influence of negative energy fields. I worked month after month, but my achievements weren't significant.

Once I had a female patient who had evidently had an evil eye cast upon her. I saw the structure of the evil eye in her energy field and thought that by removing it, I could remove the evil eye itself. At that time I didn't realize that these structures were karmic, I considered them to be a result of a negative influence of an "other". I treated all patients with similar distortions by removing these structures mechanically and the person would feel better. Shortly thereafter, however, patients appeared whose energy field deformations could not be a result of an evil eye.

For example, once a woman with a young infant came to me. I saw that the woman's and her baby's energy fields had the same structural deformations and they were caused by some particular event in the woman's life. Moreover, the mother's energy field deformations were formed several years earlier. I already knew that these kinds of deformations were related to ethical issues – they would appear when a person hates or resents someone. I could remove these deformations using magic techniques such as spells, with a gaze or with my hands. I later came to understand that what I was seeing was an information field, not a physical body field. Therefore my method of treatment remained the traditional bioenergetics approach: I'd concentrate, pass my hands over troubled areas and the deformations would disappear.

At that point I decided to test my potential, define my maximum capacity. I would schedule thirty-forty appointments a day. I was wondering how much I could withstand. The feelings were very unusual. After a week of such pressure I began feeling very tired, I would come home barely alive, my face gained a green-colored tint. Then I noticed that something was going on with my energy field, I felt as though my brain were 'boiling'. I treated the situation as a researcher would and continued working under maximum load, I didn't stop the experiment; I was really curious as to how my body would wiggle its way out of this situation. My body's choice wasn't the best... but I didn't realize that immediately.

A young woman came to see me. We had two sessions together and I removed all of her illnesses. We arranged that she would come back one more time just for reassurance. When she returned, I noticed that she had some strange changes: she had become pale, had allergic reactions and some problems with her mental state. I couldn't understand anything at that point, so I wrote down her phone number and tried to do healing at a distance over the phone. I also asked the girl's mother to write down everything that was happening in the meantime.

It was quite an extraordinary case – it was the first time when a patient's condition became worse after my influence. Itches and rashes appeared on the girl's body where I had passed my hands at a distance of twenty to thirty centimeters. When I was reading her mother's notes I, terrified, realized what was going on. What I was doing was referred to as vampirism. I was taking her energy. Having given my body the extreme overload I provoked myself to subconscious vampirism and began taking the energy from my patients. I had to stop all treatments because my body was now trained to react to any critical situation, in exactly this way – it would take another's energy. As I work distantly, I can take anybody's energy. I was gridlocked.

I decided to forget about bioenergetics forever; I saw no potential in further work. I hadn't strayed from the traditional methods of contemporary psychic/healers work, but by pushing myself to the limits for only a few days I discovered that the methods of energy "injection" and contactless massage were fruitless – they didn't give the results I had sought all my life. I could do remote healing just by the power of my will, I'd mastered all types of pressure point massage, I knew all methods for breathing techniques and nutrition. But I saw that all the methods could give only temporary relief, they would not heal a person.

The female doctor I was working with at the time, tried to support me, asking me not to jump to conclusions, advising me to have some rest and think it over. Right at that time we received an invitation from a doctor of Voznesenie Village Hospital to spend Easter with him and get some rest. I needed the time off. I also thought that after a little rest and some time to think the situation through I could make a decision. Subconsciously, I hoped that I would be given a sign as to whether I should continue my work, whether I could find a solution.

We went to Onezhskoe Lake and visited an old wooden church from the XVIth century. Easter was wonderful with fast changing weather: at the beginning it was snowing, then it started to rain, and then the sun came out and suddenly we saw a rainbow right over our heads. I went for a swim in the lake and felt myself renewed, gaining certainty that I needed to carry on doing my research. I needed to find, however, a method that would allow for healing people without any energy influence upon them. I started my search for it.

I could see a person's karmic structures and I started to influence them indirectly through the person's understanding. After finding the reasons for the karmic structure deformations I would explain them to the patient. I completely refused any energy transfer using my hands. It was a very painful period. At the beginning I couldn't master the method and the results were less satisfying than the energy work I had been doing with my hands. It took me a few months to improve the method and gradually I started to see results that I could not have achieved using the energy method. Thus I understood that this method was the future, and that, first of all, I needed to find the reasons for karmic violations, and then to examine them. I needed to study the information and pass it over to the public. I could only ever heal hundreds of people, whereas I could give an understanding of root causes of illness and paths out of it to millions.

Since then I have become a researcher, and a researcher only. Facing vampirism during treatment pushed me towards understanding that the appearance of disease is related to a violation of ethics, so treatment should be directed to comprehension of these violations and changing the person's outlook on the world. Illness is one of the paths of spiritual development. This information has been known for a very long time, we just forgot it for a while. It was given to us in sacred books many centuries ago. The main thing is to understand one's mistakes, apprehend them and, through repentance, reach harmony with the Universe, the Divine.

With my ability to see karmic structures, I can measure any healing influence. I can see the changes happening to physical and energy field structures of a person while he comprehends his actions, as the body depends on the spirit. The body, however, simultaneously has an impact on the spirit, thus treatment should be directed toward both body and soul, but first on the soul and spirit as they are primary.

The elimination of energy field deformations through comprehension and repentance gives excellent results relating to people's physical health. And since there's some time interval between the appearance of energy field deformations and an illness itself on the physical level – this method is becoming irreplaceable in early diagnosis.

Every time, I worked with patients I strove to penetrate into the essence of the illness, strove to gain an understating of what the illness was, where it came from and what its role was in the life of the person. I studied the human energy field using my hands, dowsing rod and pendulum.

In 1986 I met V.B. Polyakov, who was the head of the laboratory of bio-dynamic measurement. One of the achievements of Polyakov's school was its successful use of ponderomotoric writing[1] in medical diagnostics and its high level of accuracy achieved in both distant and contact express diagnostics of the physical field. I found something of paramount importance to me in Polyakov's method: diagnosis was the primary focus, influence was secondary.

Having mastered ponderomotoric writing, I still tried, for a while, to focus on researching illness itself, as opposed to the reasons behind it, and persistently sought information fields. By the end of 1990 I formed an opinion, that the main reason for illnesses was a breach of the energy field structure; that it was necessary to treat not a diseased organ, but the energy field. Philosophical teachings of the East confirmed the idea that the basis for the information-energy system called 'man' are the subtle energy field structures that are connected to the spirit. Subconsciously, I'd always felt this.

I saw the energy field deformations affecting the physical state of a person, saw the information structures, caused by different illnesses, influenced and corrected them and achieved the change not only of the physical state, but also of other parameters of the person's information-

---

[1] similar to automatic writing, the difference is that in automatic writing the information is presented in symbols which you can read, and in ponderomotoric writing the information is presented graphically

energy system. Step by step the elements of the system were formed. Now it enables powerful change: to treat not only already existing, but also future illness, as the deformation of energy field structures starts five-ten years before the illness appears at the physical level.

Having confirmed that deformation of the energy field causes various abnormalities on the physical level, I didn't allow myself to influence energetically. My objective was the precise diagnosis, analysis of the situation and finding the initial cause. Illness signals that a person is 'going in the wrong direction'. We're used to seeing illness as a disaster and trying to get rid of it, but illness, in fact, warns one of his mistakes and works towards his salvation. When going through pain and suffering, a person has to realize the mistakes he made, strive towards spiritual perfection and look for new ways of self-development. This inspired me to study the parameters of human spirituality.

My method of karma research can be called 'graphic clairvoyance'. I see not events themselves, but the violations of universal laws represented by them; I can see what has happened in a sort of abstract form. Knowing that the person depends on his energy field structure, I explored the relationship between behavior, ethical issues and the shape of the deformation; I would help the person through his understanding of these violations. I used the classic notion of karma, assuming that in this or one of his previous lives the person infringed on something resulting in his current sickness. As viewing previous lives of a patient is quite complicated, I was satisfied with the examination of just the present one, and the effect was much better compared to influencing energy with my hands.

However, some cases didn't quite fit in. For example, when a two-three month old child was brought to me with a serious disease, it would have been easy to say that he'd sinned in a previous life and was now suffering the consequences. But I saw that the energy field deformation of the baby would correspond to his mother's field deformations, so it was easy to conclude that the energy field structure is passed on from parents to their children.

That was the discovery of a new mechanism of information transmission by inheritance. While I was correcting the mother's field deformations, the baby was visibly recovering. I realized how much a baby's health depends on its mother's behavior, especially in the last couple of years before birth. Strong hatred experienced during pregnancy is usually a cause for the baby's traumas or illness of organs located on the child's head: for example, some sort of problem with vision or hearing. On the other hand, if a mother feels strongly offended during pregnancy, the baby will be easily offended in the future. The mother's behavior defines the destiny and the health of her baby. At the beginning I didn't pay much attention to the father's behavior and, only later, I understood that both the mother and the father are equally responsible for their baby's body and spirit. Parents pass on complete information about their behavior and the behavior of their ancestors to their children. A child's destiny, body, character and spirituality are formed of this information.

Every discovery obtained through my research shows with greater and greater clarity the unity of the surrounding world, of living and inanimate nature, of lower and higher organisms. I have to say that I always felt this way and everything happening around me often confirmed this unity. I spent my childhood on the coast of the Azov Sea. I watched minnows frolic in shallow water, schools of them would come to the surface and perform their dance, gliding vertically on the tips of their tails. That kind of playfulness was only possible in the children of intelligent creatures, strange and unknown to us.

Once, while fishing I had the opportunity to observe a 'suicidal fish'. Coming closer to the shore I saw a small fish on the shore that was hardly breathing, not too far from the water line. I was just about to put it back in the water when it suddenly jumped, its scales sparkled and it disappeared back into the river. A couple minutes later the leap onto the shore was repeated, and then again back into the water.

I was intrigued and started to follow it. It was the same fish and it was discovering something new about the surrounding world in such a strange way. Persistently it jumped out onto the beach and then again back into the river, repeatedly risking it's life – it could have easily run out of breath or accidentally jump in the wrong direction, away from the water. But the fish continued jumping back and forth, never making a mistake.

Hasn't everyone come across a warning from an animal at least once? When I worked as a guide on Ritza lake, I once saw a snake that had been beaten with stones lying on the path. I felt sorry for it so I picked it up and put it in a plastic bag to set it free somewhere in the woods far away from people. The snake wasn't long, with whitish skin, and for some reason, I thought it wasn't poisonous. It was sluggishly lying in the bag, showing no activity and I started to get used to it. Forgetting that it might be dangerous, I occasionally touched it with my finger. It was inert for a long time and then, suddenly, with a slight turn of its head, it bit through the plastic bag.

I understood that this was a warning. I took it away from the path and set it free in the grass. The snake started moving slowly, crawling under the stones, and I started playfully holding it back by its tail. The snake was patiently looking back waiting for me to let it go but I kept holding it. Suddenly, as quick as lightning, the snake coiled up and its head appeared right next to my hand. It was looking at me, not even trying to bite, but warning.

It was such a surprise when a couple days later, during training I saw a picture of the familiar snake – it was the deadly, poisonous, Kaznakov viper, an inhabitant of the Caucasus Mountains.

One of the first cases, where I managed to change not only the physical, but psychological state of a patient was as follows. A young woman was in love with a young man, but for some reason they could not be together and so they broke up. For a few years after the break up, this love tortured her – not even the love itself, but something strange, something agonizing. She realized that she shouldn't be so attached to him, but the attachment existed and was destroying her. It was more like a spell than love. The woman had been meeting other young men hoping that she would like one of them. She had no such luck ...

I began examining whether this was her own fault. The result of the testing was: no. Who else could possibly be responsible? A woman, a relative, her grandmother...

To my surprise, the woman knew what I was talking about. When her grandmother was young she was in love with a young man, but married another for status. The grandmother had killed the love in herself and in the young man. Thus the granddaughter had to pay the grandmother's debt through suffering. The grandmother, having received this information, realized that by killing love, she had violated supreme laws and the girl was set free from her suffering. I understood that this method was good, not only for curing people, but for helping their souls, for correcting their destinies.

Those of you, who are at least somewhat familiar with the esoteric literature and philosophies of the East, have certainly come across the one hundred and eight laws that govern the Universe. I tried to find them in the literature many times, but, unfortunately, I still haven't succeeded in finding all of them in complete form – perhaps it's not given to us to know them all yet...

My experience working in bioenergetics shows that among the many different violations people commit in their downtrodden, down-to-earth daily lives, the most severe is killing love in any manifestation. All the other violations are secondary and are the consequence of the lack of man's love to God, the Universe, relatives, children, nature and people...

The following instance strengthened my conviction that karma diagnostics would allow for the treatment of people's souls. I was addressed by a woman who occasionally suffered from strange urges –she would get a strong desire to jump out of the window, commit suicide, and she'd get an irresistible longing to die. She would ask her relatives to tie her to the bed and hold her. These urges were getting stronger and would appear more and more frequently. The woman was afraid that she wouldn't manage to hold on and it would come to a terrible end.

My examination of this case showed that a violation of the supreme laws had been committed by her mother. She was deeply loved by one man, but she treated him with no respect. She was pleased that another person was totally dependent on her. Her mother was killing the life and love in this man; her words, thoughts and actions created a program of destruction that returned now to her daughter.

The return of negative programs sometimes happens slowly, and not always to the responsible party, but quite often to his relatives and descendants. After this woman talked with her mother, and her mother recognized her guilt, the urges stopped. I understood how much the virtues and flaws of our parents, brothers and sisters are connected with our health, mentality and fate.

Each new communication with my patients led to the discovery of new elements of the system that I now call the 'system of energy field self-regulation'.

The self-regulating energy field system is a feedback loop with the Universe. The essence of it is that any kind of human action, whether it's positive or negative, due to the unity of the universe's information-energy field, returns back to the person.

We constantly hear that positive actions are rewarded and negative actions are punished, but somehow we don't see an increase in kindness nor a decrease in evil. One of the best explanations, from my point of view, is given by the St. Augustine, who said that God always punishes evil, but because this process takes some time, the person has enough time to do more wrong things before he receives his punishment. This explanation corresponds perfectly to the mechanism of transmission of information through the energy field structures.

The self-regulating energy field doesn't recognize individuals – it just sees a negative process that must be stopped. The blocking mechanism starts automatically. In earlier times, this mechanism of punishment would stretch over several generations and would manifest as illness and misfortune in the grandchildren or great-grandchildren's generations or in the next incarnations of the person. These days the process is sped up, so the person himself pays for his wrong-doing throughout his present life and through the health and well-being of his children.

Retribution through children's health seems ridiculous from a regular persons point of view, however, there are no people on the energy field level, only ideas; and every person is an aggregate of particular programs. The blocking mechanism works against the negative ideas and programs that are dangerous for the Universe. Children reinforce their parents programs, therefore the price they must pay is higher. However, during the last five years personal responsibility has become a larger part of the equation. So far I don't understand the reasons for this trend.

A child is like a magnifying glass for the shortcomings of the adult world. A lot of people noticed that children start to misbehave in their parents' presence, while they behave themselves with everybody else. In most cases this is the work of the same karmic mechanism. While the child is communicating with his parents all the positive and negative programs the parents passed on to their kid are activated and amplified.

Recently, studying different problems, I discovered that not only do children inherit their parents' karma, but also that parents are responsible, on the energy field level, for their child's behavior and actions. These days, child's thoughts and actions affect the energy field starting at the age of eight and a half – from this age they influence their parents' spirit, destiny and health. About two thousand years ago this process didn't start until the child reached thirteen-fourteen years old.

When I began studying and clearing my karma I stopped getting ill, but a new problem surfaced. My energy rapidly increased as did its impact. This made it very difficult for me to balance myself. However, it was necessary, as my being even a tiny bit offended with somebody, would have a great impact on that person's health and destiny.

I was hoping that if I could solve this problem everything would be fine. Through constant work I got rid of negative emotions, hatred, resentment, but then I encountered an even more serious problem. I had to start controlling people around me, as even a small resentment directed towards me would become a real danger for them.

This helped me understand one of the underlying reasons for Russia's tragedy. A person with a clear or "closed" karma is closely coupled with the Divine, therefore aggression against this person also works against the Universe. If a person attacks someone on his own behalf, he pays for it himself, but if he represents society, the society is held responsible. In the 1920's Lenin issued an order obliterating the clergy, monks and demolishing all sanctuaries and monasteries – this was equivalent to attacking the Universe. After that, inevitably, a burst of crime and violence had to follow. The society paid with millions of lost lives for breaching the highest ethical laws.

The memory of society's mistakes forms a part of each one of us. All sins and misfortunes of society are stored in each individual's subconscious, his karma. We still haven't forgotten the Soviet song "We will destroy the world of violence..." In fact on the energy-field level, this song caries a powerful destructive program towards the future and the Universe.

Very often, people come to me asking for help with their children's enuresis. I always explain that enuresis is only the tip of the iceberg. Usually, enuresis appears as a result of the mother suppressing her love for a man. If this suppression was strong and happened for a long time, a deformation forms in the energy field of her first chakra. As a result, her children might not only have enuresis, but also possible dysfunctions and problems in their personal lives, heart disease, or illnesses related to their heads. Enuresis may also be the result of an earlier abortion, as in this case the woman also kills love.

When mothers don't know about these reasons they often seek out a psychotherapist or hypnotherapist who suggests a subconscious block that stops the enuresis. The program of destroying love and life is still there, however. So now that the mechanism of blocking incorrect personal behavior has been removed, one can expect that the child will fulfill an even greater program of destroying the love than the mother.

A woman often visited doctors complaining about not feeling well, but tests revealed nothing, so, from the doctors point of view, she had no reason to feel bad. Repeated visits to different "witch doctors" would not bring her any relief – they would see a powerful evil eye, but they couldn't help her. They would even start being ill themselves after contact with her. I took a close look at what was happening and discovered that it was a "reflexive evil eye" which is indeed impossible to remove using folk remedies.

"You wanted something bad to happen to your coworker", I explained. "And this is the reason for your condition now. Your program, designed to bring harm, has returned back to you and has deformed your energy field. How is your coworker? Is she feeling well?"

"She is on sick leave, but it's her child that is ill, not herself."

I examined the coworker and her child's energy fields. Both of them had this program designed to harm in their energy fields. This is why the child was ill, he was more vulnerable.

"It's your responsibility that her child is sick. Do you have children also?"

"Yes, I have a son."

I examined her son's energy field and found the same program creating a strong deformation.

That was a typical example how we destroy ourselves, our children and people around us, without even knowing it.

When I just started my research of karmic structures, a woman approached me. She had suddenly started experiencing severe headaches, and her overall health wasn't brilliant.

"Five days ago you were wishing harm on your husband and it was a very strong emotion."

"That's impossible, because I love my husband and would never do something like this to him."

I insisted that I was right.

"You had an ill wish towards him. It was a significant, powerful evil wish about five days ago in the evening."

"How could it be? He was late from work, about two hours, and I worried about him."

I realized what had happening.

"What did you feel at that time?"

"All these crazy (nonsense) came to my mind."

"You have to understand, when you think that something negative can happen, you actually invite this into one's life. Moreover, the more realistic your thoughts the greater damage you are evoking. Strong discipline of our mind is highly important now, especially because today we hold a high level of energy. Not inflicting any harm is one of the most important laws of the Universe even in our thoughts. This can't just be an abstract principle - this should become a way of living.

The research I conduct every day using extrasensory diagnostics testifies that following ethical norms is a necessary condition and is indeed the only path to survival. It's also the best protection. We look around in search for threats around us, while the main threat bides its time, invisible, inside us. The root of this problem is a lack of understanding of the surrounding world: of ourselves and what happens to us; incorrect behavior which invisibly leads to the internal disintegration of a person. The catastrophes and horrors that we fight all the time are the result of spiritual deficiencies. Any effort directed towards fighting the shadows, the consequences, cannot remove the main cause, the spiritual disintegration that is happening now, which, incidentally is rarely connected to our suffering.

My next story opened a new facet in my research. A woman called me and said that she was having serious problems connected to strange and incomprehensible events. She constantly felt powerful pressure on her psyche from outside. Everybody who tried to help her would find themselves in trouble or ill. Once this woman found a clairvoyant "witch doctor", who shook her head and said "I doubt I can help you". The visit brought relief for one day, but after that everything came back.

I started to heal her. Quickly enough she started to feel better, the strange influence stopped; however, I noticed that my relatives started falling ill, all with the same symptoms: weakness and joint pain. I began searching for the source and found that it was the "work" of the person who was harming my patient. As I'd been working with bioenergetics for a while, when it came to my family, it was tempting to use what's called "magic" to stop the culprit. I was facing a choice of which way to go.

It wasn't easy for me to refuse use of force, especially because my many years of work in the bioenergetic area and study of esoteric literature, presented a large array of such tactics. Nevertheless, I decided to try avoiding answering forcefully, hurting this person. Instead, I decided to help him.

When somebody becomes the victim of an energy attack, the reason for this could be his personal fault or that of his ancestors. If one responds with an energy attack, it causes a chain reaction, because an energy stroke is a flagrant violation that leads to new punishment.

Can this person be rescued? Further extrasensory testing shows that the person attacking my patient wasn't guilty himself. The main source of all that was happening with this woman was contained in her personal karma. When her grandmother was young she fell in love with a man, but didn't want to have a child and had an abortion. Killing love and a child resulted in her daughter, granddaughter and descendants having to pay for her deed. Moreover everybody had it in different forms – illnesses, ruined destinies, mental problems.

When I refused to respond with an energy attack, I won a victory over myself – in difficult circumstances, when I was so tempted to respond with force I managed not to go down that path. That was my victory, after which I understood, once and for all, that I have no right, under any circumstances, to answer violence with violence. After studying the principles of the system of energy field self-regulation in more detail, I saw the possible consequences of "justified" use of force.

Many aspects of civil law don't correspond to Universal law. If somebody hits me and I hit him back as is my right, it doesn't mean that I can do the same on the energy field level. These are completely different levels. If I were to respond by hitting him back, only he would suffer. With an energy attack, however, since every person is connected with his children and relatives on the energy field level, the blow affects the entire line. In response there's a counter attack – punishment for the one who dealt the blow and his family line.

I realized that the increase in human potential energy requires close attention to behavior, emotions and thoughts. You can't thoughtlessly make any categorical statements, as this already has an effect. I understood why the Bible talks about meekness and humility – it's really about curbing ones energy potential.

Then how come sorcerers and magicians use different methods of influence, including force? Having thought about it for a while, I realized that they only see a small part without seeing the whole, so they cure only the lowest levels of the energy field and physical body, casting all deformations from a single part to the whole. This just postpones the illness. Compared to saints who could – due to their high ethics – rise to understand the true reasons and relationships of events to see the whole, sorcerers work only in the specific niche defined by them, that's why often they have a limited "specialization". The main point is that people who practice magic have always possessed ability and a relatively clear karma, so the violations they commit while using magic are not blocked right away, instead they accumulate over time and their descendants have to deal with the consequences.

I examined what happens when a psychic or sorcerer removes negative energy from a sick person. There's a lot of different methods that can be used for this purpose: it can be sent into water, plants, wax figures, pets, a division of healthy strong soldiers, the center of the Earth, space or it can be burned in different ways. This energy, containing a charge of aggression, enters the energy field of the object that it was thrown at, deforms it, and automatically returns to the "healer's" energy field and that of his relatives.

Any type of healing that is not based on spiritual development leads to degradation. Removing some symptoms doesn't signify a cure.

Recently a woman asked me:

"Three months ago you helped my acquaintance and now her fibroma has disappeared completely. I couldn't even imagine that just by asking for forgiveness, somebody can get rid of such an illness."

"This doesn't surprise me. The method is constantly refining itself and now not only the functional condition of a patient can improve, often even organic disorders disappear. Results depend on my correct understanding of the cause-and-effect mechanism and determination of the real origin of the illness, on my spiritual and physical state at the moment, on the condition of the patient's karma and on the degree of his understanding of his violations."

When I just started my practice I was living a regular life: eating meat, drinking vodka, often getting irritated – while I was curing patients using non-invasive massage. Later, when I could see the results of this kind of work I changed a lot in my lifestyle and my behavior. A day before my sessions with patients I consume a minimum amount of food and nothing at all on the day.

Sometimes I get so carried away by diagnostics and development of the method's potential, that I forget about the risk. One must always be extra cautious while working on the subtle energy field levels.

Not too long ago my acquaintance asked me to consult a woman. I had about forty minutes of free time and I agreed. The women who entered was very elegant and confident, she sat down and looked at me with curiosity. She had a lot of problems. Powerful egoism and excessive striving towards material welfare were the reasons for the beginnings of sickness. It is very difficult to help this kind of patient because skepticism and a lack of trust closes them off from me.

I was explaining the reasons for her misfortune while she tried to make a discussion out of our session. Nevertheless, I had to convince her - these kinds of challenges help me find new reasons and explanations for the causes of illnesses.

"If one cell of the organism takes everything for itself," I explained, "it lives well for a while, but then its actions start to destroy the organism and eventually they die together. Egoism is normal to a certain degree, but a person who thinks only of himself is trying to kill God and the Universe. Of course this can't last forever. Sooner or later the programs destroying the Universe have to be blocked by disease, injuries and misfortune."

"So what are you suggesting? You want me to believe in God?"

"Believing in God is your own business. I am just describing the reasons for your illness. You don't have to believe in God, but you have to love the Universe and it's soul. Egoism, limitless striving towards material welfare kills the most important feeling – love. You're carrying a program of destroying the Universe in your energy field and worse, you don't want to stop it."

We resumed our verbal duel. I ran out of arguments to convince her but I started a process called "karma clearing". Her energy field was cleared. However, not only did I not feel satisfaction, I got a very unpleasant feeling.

The woman treated everything as entertainment.

"You are saying that we can't only take care of material things, but our life forces us to do so."

"I had a lot of opportunities to make a lot of money, but if I had taken them I would have had to sacrifice my research. Now I am forty and I live with my family of four in a fourteen square meter room in a communal apartment, but I have this opportunity to help you. And not only you, but myself as well. When material welfare is more important than spiritual needs – it's momentary wealth at the expense of spiritual death. Imagine yourself sitting in a restaurant where everything is on fire and you are calmly finishing your meal. For a lot of people what is on the plate in front of them is more important than what is happening around them."

"Do you heal everybody like this?"

"Yes, the first step is understanding. However, even if it looks easy, it's a very dangerous exercise."

"For you or for me?"

"First of all - for me"

"What do you mean?"

"Look, your program of destroying the Universe was 550 points and your illness was - 350. Now your illness is zero, but the program of destruction is 350. That means that I healed your body, but not your spirit, meaning that I violated the main principle – to heal by understanding."

I pictured myself before and after this meeting – on the energy field level one of my lungs, my liver and the bottom of my abdomen were completely black.

"I have to pay for not being able to explain the cause of your illness."

"And what are you going to do?"

"I will try to find a way to convince you. If I can find a reason for why I couldn't accomplish it before – I will have my health back, if not – I will have to pay."

Right at that moment I realized the mistake I made.

"I should have just given you the complete information I received about your condition, but I felt sorry for you. Did I tell you that you might have some other diseases if you don't restore harmony?"

"Yes."

"Do you know that you have the beginnings of womb cancer?"

"I always had a presentiment about it and accepted that. I am ready to die calmly."

"Your 'heroic' death won't change anything. You will leave your program for disintegrating the universe for your kids to deal with. You must think, not about your worthy death, but about salvation for your spirit and your children.

We sat in silence for a while and I saw that, finally, her energy field deformations started to smooth out. The woman's aura, which had been covered with a black stain began to fill up with shimmering light.

"Now your program of destroying the Universe is zero and your disease is zero. Also my lungs and liver are clear now."

I didn't say anything else to this woman. There was no oncology in her energy field anymore. She understood that by feeling love toward the Universe and God, leaving dissatisfaction with the surrounding world behind, one can save oneself from any serious disease.

A woman came for a session and told me her story with tears in her eyes.

"I got divorced from my husband, our life together was dreadful, I felt that he had a negative influence on me, something was happening to my sanity. When we finally got divorced I felt much better even with three kids on my own, I even started singing. We didn't see each other for half a year, but he came to visit not too long ago. Right away I started to feel not well, my daughter started crying hysterically, my son got enuresis, and my second daughter fell ill. Could this be related to his visit?

It didn't take me long to figure out what was happening.

"Unfortunately, what has happened to your family is not an accident. Your spouse is a "vampire", he takes the children's energy, destiny and health, negatively influences their characters, and inserts his negative programs into their energy fields. He's an egotistical person. Such a massive seizure of energy from kids represents that his karma is very negative. Judging by his energy field he has a strong disconnect from the Cosmos and from love, much inner aggression, egoism, disintegration of the soul, therefore he must become a "vampire". This is a classic example. Vampirism can be found in both his father & mother's familial lines. What happened to your children can be removed quickly, however, in the future it is better for them to stay away from their father."

My analysis shows that vampirism is a serious illness, because it destroys a person's soul and is passed on to descendants. Also the consequences of vampirism don't appear right away, sometimes the process of disintegration can take a few generations.

The basis for vampirism is an incorrect outlook on the world. A girl asked me whether she was charging her energy correctly when she imagined a stream of blue fire entering her. I took a look at her karmic structures during this action and found that this was a violation of the law of the Universe.

Any kind of deliberate energy intake – from nature, Cosmos, the Sun – is a sign that this person is lacking energy and needs to get it from somewhere. This is a prerequisite for the development of vampirism. The major mistake here is that the person, instead of connecting energy and spirituality, separates them.

When we feel love toward the Universe we receive an enormous amount of energy. To receive enough energy you have to get to the highest levels of energy – spirituality, nobleness, love - you have to live on these terms. As soon as we start thinking abstractedly about energy, separating energy from spirituality and ethics, we condemn our spiritual structures to poverty, by filling only our physical body with energy. People have to know that the energy they receive through subtle feelings heals their body, destiny and soul. A mechanical approach and focusing on obvious-gross energy will lead to deformations in the subtle spiritual structures. Consumerism in any form will lead to degradation.

Another example just came to my mind. A young fellow was taught how to charge his body with energy from the Universe. A few times a day he would practice this technique, and at the end he started to take energy from his teacher. The outcome was dismal – the deformation of his spiritual structures started.

I got an idea, to examine what kind of effect the same exercise would have had on a person two thousand years ago. The examination disclosed that these parameters were very high. That means that in earlier years this exercise worked wonderfully, however, as you can't enter the same river twice, it is impossible to use the old techniques endlessly. We tend to forget that not only man has changed, but the surrounding world has also changed. Physical methods of self-development are not effective anymore, now spiritual self-development is mandatory. Time is not a linear category, and if the speed of all processes has increased so much, it means that the energy structure of the surrounding world must have changed as well. Nevertheless we behave as if nothing has happened, and try to rely on old knowledge and methods.

The more I learned about the potential of this method of empirical testing the more its complications became apparent. I realized that it was impossible to use it as I had originally planned, to form a group of individuals and teach them how to work. This method is so closely connected to morality, ethics and spiritual parameters that it places a lot of limitations on the person attempting to use it and not everybody can bear these limitations.

I connect to the karmic structure of my patients, therefore if I have analogous violations to the ones I am trying to remove in my own field, I must eliminate them from myself first of all. That's why every time, before I begin working with a patient I check whether I have the right to heal him and if the answer is no, first, I clean and "close" my own karma using prayer. After a few months of working with patients I have to carry out a deep, fundamental cleansing and fasting. And even this is not enough. It turns out, that if a healer wants to be effective in treating people without harming himself and his patients, his karma must be "blocked", and nobody from today's army of healers has this quality. You can't close your karma with a healer's diploma, you need to constantly clear and strengthen your spirit by disconnecting from everything that can "tie a person down to earth". This is necessary not only for the healer, but also for every person, especially in recent times.

One morning a woman had a consultation with me, and the day after she started to feel unwell. She got a strong headache and nausea.

"Were you upset with your husband yesterday evening around 7pm?"

"Sure, he got into a car accident and now the car is all wrecked. I was ok at the moment, but I had a lot to say to him that evening."

"While undergoing karmic diagnostics and treatments there is a strong and deep influence that takes place. For a certain period of time, until the energy field stabilizes and balance is achieved, the patient is absolutely prohibited from experiencing any negative emotions. Energy field structures are harmonized and restored at the moment of contact with the Divine and any negative emotion creates massive distortions. Approaching God – is not a piece of cake that always brings pleasure, but a very complex, responsible and necessary process.

My next story is directly related to what is happening in the world at the moment.

"Inside I always had this longing for Divinity, and I used to get in trouble if I lost my connection with it. Twice I almost died," a man told me. "The connection between rejection of the Divine and punishment was so obvious that I couldn't call it an accident. I had a clear understanding: God punished me."

"You are right and I can explain, in detail, how the system of punishment works and show the reason for your misfortune," I suggested. "Somebody said, even though the clock was invented by man it doesn't mean that man is inside of every clock. The universe is created by God and is controlled by Him, but it doesn't mean that every punishment is sent by him "personally", because He controls the universe using the laws He created. There is a magnificent mechanism of energy field self-regulation. What people often relegate to the "mystical" can always, in reality be analyzed.

"You are the third, unplanned and unwanted child in the family. That's why your parents unconsciously passed on their program of your destruction to you, which transformed into a program of self-destruction. From your childhood you had a relatively low vitality and you used to get sick often. You were born in these circumstances because in your previous lives you rejected love to your children. By looking at your energy field and karmic structures you had no chance of staying alive. The only way for you to survive was the powerful aspiration for the Divine and highest feelings. Your subconscious mind always knew about it and was pulling you in the right direction, but your conscious mind worked accordingly to another program. As soon as you rejected the direction of salvation, your destiny structures would start falling apart and you would get very close to facing death. Why didn't you die?

Because you were rejecting God and spirituality only in your conscious mind, that's why you weren't killed in a fight and didn't die in a car accident. This is evidence that your program of rejection didn't pass into the subconsciousness, meaning that the destiny structures hadn't fallen apart completely. If your focus on rejection were to become permanent it would pass into your subconscious mind and that would trigger blockage of disintegration, which in turn could manifest as incurable illness, or serious injury with physical suffering."

Why would his death have to be so difficult? Because physical and spiritual suffering helps clear the subconscious. How does it work? The only way to bear suffering is to rise above it using the spirit, to transfer the point of focus from the body to the spirit. This is a natural process that happens automatically. A suffering person becomes more spiritual. My studies of the mechanism of transferring energy field information allow me to say that humanity is in the same situation now and there is a similar "blocking" mechanism in place for the human race.

I studied the karma of humanity. Entering these structures is very dangerous. The most important violation of law humanity commits is the rejection of the Divine, immersion in the pragmatic, starting in the 10th century. This violation is present in the energy field of every person living on Earth now.

The karma of the Russian "socialist" society, contains extra negative programs in addition to those mentioned above: the program of destroying people, men and women due to a strong attachment to material wealth which began between 1929 and 1937; the program of hatred towards people which began at the end of the 19th century; the program of destroying fathers, brothers and sons due to the same attachment to material wealth. That's why life in our country is so difficult. If we don't understand, make sense of these programs and free ourselves from them, then we will endlessly repatriate / privatize our factories and manufacturing plants until we pay for these programs with our suffering.

Here's the path I took beginning at studying magic and sorcery, through non-traditional medicine and ethics to attaining a new understanding of the world.

The basis of the Universe is information: "In the beginning was the Word".

What we call the Universe, from my point of view, resulted from the extraction of two components: matter and an information field from Unity (which always existed and which we call God). Each of them contains the opposite component in non-manifest form. The main condition for these opposites to exist is their constant mutual transition from one to the other. The field strives to become matter, and matter strives to become the field.

The accumulation of energy connections in matter is a sign of the transition of the material component to information. The opposite process can be expressed as an increase in density of matter, mass or as increased complexity. Energy connections are also information –the more connections, the more information. Matter, as it were, becomes "spiritual". Information becomes energy, and energy becomes matter.

If we take a look at the solar system, the purpose of its existence is the creation of more complex elements on the Sun, the creation of the multifaceted information connections due to the appearance of new planets, and the creation of complex information structures on planets based on organics, as a new step in increasing information density. The purpose of the existence of any star-system is creation of life. What we call "spirit" is above the information field and matter.

When matter reaches a certain level of density it transforms into information. Singularity (the state of matter, concentrated in a single point) is the Universe. The subtle levels of the energy field – are the absence of matter, time and space, i.e. a point. A point strives to become infinity and infinity strives to become the point. Every point of the Universe has non-manifest information about the entire Universe; in other words, a point is non-manifested infinity, and infinity is the non-manifested point.

There are two theories of the origin of stars. According to the first one – by Kant-Laplace – they appear as a result of the thickening of interstellar space. The second one – by the academic Ambarcumian – talks about the appearance of stars out of "black holes". A young star's instability, the massive explosive processes happening inside of them – based on the author's theory – are all evidence of the presence of proto-substances inside of them.

Based on the concept stated above and my research we can consider the origin of stars as a dialectical process of the transition of information into matter, also as a result of "fertilization" of an interstellar substance by an information block. This informational block can be realized as the matter from a "black hole". The emergence of stars is a result of interaction between two origins: the manifest and non-manifest Universe. The processes that occur inside stars and inside living organisms are identical. These are processes of transition of energy into matter and vice versa.

The development of the Universe is the breach of unity on the physical/material level and an increase of unity on the information-field level; differentiation and increasing variety on the physical level together with greater identity on the energy field level. At a certain stage of development, the differences between the physical and energy field components disappear and then a new phase of development begins.

Hence, there is a contradiction: the Universe remains a point on the subtle, energy field level and, simultaneously, widens, creating new matter, time and space. Development follows the pendulum principle: the direction of movement changes from information unity – to physical separation.

Any object in the Universe can be considered a process, at the same time, any process is also an object. Any process or object oscillates between information identity to physical differentiation. Physical differentiation has to strictly conform to spiritual unity. The main condition for development of these two opposites is the presence of a third party, which catalyzes the non-manifest presence of one opposite in the other. This role is fulfilled by "energy" the intermediary determining the Universe's development.

Information, energy and matter all compose a whole. An understanding of this has existed in human culture for a long time – for example, in Christianity this is represented by the Holy Trinity (God-Father, God-Son and God-Holy Spirit).

Any object by developing, repeats the cycle of the Universe's development. While staying absolutely united on the subtle energy field level, the object differentiates itself on the physical level. Differentiation on the physical level is necessarily preceded by corresponding development on the spiritual level, which guarantees stability during physical separation. This demonstrates a clear priority of the spiritual. In this way, the law of unity and the struggle of opposites would look like this: the existing "nothing" extracts its own opposite, in order to become "something" completely new.

Let's move on to the question of the origin of life. The more differentiated the physical world the more unified the energy fields, starting with the subtle levels and graduating to the denser ones. Inner unity begins to appear on the external level, the form starts to reflect the content. Unity begins to appear on levels that have never been unified before.

With increasing heterogeneity the level of unity in a limited space builds up to the point that an object emerges from, is separated from the Universe. Bringing the object up to the level of unity represented by the surrounding world signifies its death. The density of information increases to the point that there's an opposition between the object and the surrounding world.

We can say that all life in the Universe appeared simultaneously and, at the same time, is a single organism, which continues to differentiate itself with all its components in constant connection and interaction with each other. The development of this process and further physical differentiation is only possible when the primary orientation is towards inner information unity. Matter, time and space are external forms; information and spirit – are the content. Content is manifest in form and form develops content.

The basis of any object's life is oscillation between informational and physical processes. Human life is a reflection of the Universe in miniature, and since time and space are compressed in human beings, the transition of information into matter happens faster. Living objects are unique in the degree of unity and the speed of transition of information into matter (information becomes energy and energy becomes matter). It's likely that increasing the unity and speed of mutual transition is the point of the development of a living object.

The higher the degree of inner unity, density of information, the more an organism detaches itself from the surrounding world. This is what we call the development of consciousness and individuality. The process of physical separation from the surrounding world is possible only if unity with the Universe increases. The process of unity with the Universe is what we call culture; the process of separation is what we call civilisation. Culture gives birth to civilisation. First, civilisation rejects culture, but later, like a prodigal son, returns back to it to avoid destruction, only to repeat this process again, but at a higher level with increased amplitude. If the return to culture is not on the appropriate spiritual level this leads to the downfall of civilisation. The rejection of unity and Love – the feeling that manifests unity in the Universe – leads to the end of civilisation.

It is well accepted that the essence of the law of unity and the struggle of opposites is reconciliation without mutual destruction. The main condition for these opposites to reconcile is their ability to transition into each other, which allows them to increase their degree of unity. The main difference between living and inanimate matter is in the speed of transition of opposites into each other; the purpose of life is to increase the manifestation of spirit in matter resulting from an increase in the speed of their mutual transition.

Let's go back to the pendulum. For a certain frequency there are two states that exclude each other – the pendulum's deviation from the vertical line to the right and to the left. These two opposing states can subsist without destroying each other only because they are separated in time. An attempt to combine them, for example within one second while the period of oscillation is five seconds, will lead to bringing the motion to a halt, the discontinuation of development. Now let's imagine that the frequency of the pendulum's oscillation increases to a few oscillations per second. That means combining these two opposing states without their mutual destruction.

Life on Earth emerged as a way to preserve the level of unity with the Sun that detached different planets from itself. That is, the level of physical identity decreased and the level of informational unity rose as a way to compensate for physical separation. Therefore, in the final analysis, there is no separation overall. Any object in the Universe strives to emit something that is opposite to itself on the physical level, that simultaneously strengthens the unity with it on the informational level. This develops the system as a whole. A mother giving birth to a child is the same as a star giving birth to a planet. Physical detachment has to be compensated by spiritual unity.

Life on Earth confirms the implementation of unity between the Sun and a new planet. The Solar system strives to maximize its physical differentiation, on one hand, and, on the other hand, to retain informational unity. Life, as it appeared on Earth, develops in accordance to the same laws. On the physical level, the formation of a new species takes place, the diversity of forms increases, meanwhile, on the energy field level, the degree of unity rises. Life on Earth not only appeared as a whole organism, but also continues to exist as a whole organism, and is controlled by the system of self-regulation that is realized on the information-energy level. The purpose of this system is to support the appropriateness of each part's behavior to the interests of the whole. The higher the energy potential of one node the more it must focus on the center. If the connection with the center lags, but the autonomy of the nodes increases, the entire system can perish. Therefore, the rejection of the nodes that break the unity of the system is unavoidable.

The behavior of the object has to correspond to the informational structures of the entire organism. If the physical, emotional or the informational behavior of the object deviates from the programs laid down in the information field of the system, then the system's energy field will attack the object's energy field. The energy field of this object gets deformed and the program of destruction is implemented, in other words, the program returns the object to its initial state. This could be a singular object or a group, responsible for the disturbance of the law of unity. In medical terms – the health of the body is determined by its spiritual health.

The information field takes priority over the human body and determines its fate, character and physical state. Hence, we can say that the main precondition of good physical health is the knowledge and compliance with the laws of the information field of the Universe – laws of Unity, Spirituality and Love.

Presently the speed of all processes on Earth has risen so much that the immediate escalation of physical adaptation is required. The biogenosphere changes rapidly.

Since the information processes in the Universe are primary in relation to the physical ones, physical adaptation is directly related, first of all, to influencing the informational, spiritual structures of human beings. This explains the popularity of magic, occultism, yoga and various religious trends. People welcome any new Messiah or Guru with delight, when he promises salvation and new truth. Everybody expects to have ready solutions, but they forget that hard and painful inner work is compulsory for revival. The essence of this work is known to humanity - it is a striving to understand the world around us, examine its laws and behave according to them.

The energy level of humanity has increased sharply in recent years. What used to be achieved due to years of hard work can now be achieved within a few months. The increase in man's potential can be compared to the change from riding a bicycle to piloting an airplane. However, it will be difficult to use this potential if the mentality of humankind remains the mentality of a biker, without changing to the mentality of a pilot. The psychological level of a regular person and one who received access to high energy with the potential to influence living and inanimate objects must differ even more.

My research shows that, these days not only physical acts or strong emotions can harm living and inanimate nature, even a careless thought can do this. With the increased energy potential of man, the consequences of negative interaction rise in geometric progression. The information-energy influence on living and inanimate objects can be very dangerous.

Aggression towards one person is the program of destruction of his children and relatives. Negative influence returns back to the initiator and his relatives, due to the mechanism of self-regulation of the energy fields. The psychological training of humanity lags far behind its energy potential; we can say that, in fact, humanity is now in the process of self-destruction. The results of this can be seen already.

What is the reason for this tragic inconsistency between man's psychology and the reality of the surrounding world? The Psychology of modern Western civilization is very pragmatic, and the majority of the world's population subscribes to this worldview. A major point is placed on the realization of information, instead of its accumulation. Consequently, the ineffective and "low profit" process of understanding the world and the creation of new concepts and ethical structures is left out of the collective intent. Ready-to-use recipes with maximum practical results are preferred to the hard and long process of understanding.

If we analyze the development of any religion, magic or yoga, we will see the following main phases in common:

- *comprehension of the world in the present moment, which happens through the denial of surroundings, overcoming one's dependence on them and the refusal to interact with them.*
- *discovering the laws of world development and creating a system of behavior which reflects these laws;*
- *practical application of obtained knowledge.*

Before this process could stretch over centuries and thousands of years, and people could not see or comprehend it as a whole. It is similar to the blind men from the well known parable, who by touching the different parts of the elephant tried to figure out what it was. Today humanity has a chance to see this process as a whole in all its unity and integrity.

Presently the process of disconnection dominates in the spiritual search. There are some schools that focus only on the first step – information accumulation. This is an escape from reality, rejection of civilization as it is, and denial of the two following steps. Hare Krishnas would be a great example.

The second group of schools focuses on the return to principals of ethics, righteous behavior – this path is represented by various religions.

The third path focuses on using practical results and neglects learning and ethics – this is represented by magic and sorcery.

An interesting transformation happened within extra sensory studies. Beginning with the elements of knowledge and ethics, this path rapidly degraded when its representatives started to receive financial rewards, and is now oriented towards magic and sorcery. This is quite a natural and logical trend – without love for God any process of comprehension turns into a desire for wealth.

Now we can see the accelerated development of all processes. This allows us to see "the elephant" as a whole. Now we can imagine and understand the processes that define the present human condition and the challenges that it faces.

The main condition for survival at the moment is the unification of that which was previously impossible to combine, using dialectics. In particular: the renunciation of the earthly, unity with Cosmos and obtaining information, and then the embodiment of its moral laws and the practical implementation of this information on all levels.

"You can't worship God and mammon at the same time" said Jesus. Two thousand years ago, the combination of these opposing tendencies was impossible within the life of one person. Now the world has changed, the frequency of oscillation of the pendulum has changed without causing mutual annihilation of the opposites, that is, the speed of transition of information and matter into each other. Therefore, we can say that a person who is destined to survive in the near future has to be a saint and a businessman simultaneously.

Two opposing processes have to coexist in every person's consciousness: one of them – the rejection of the world, striving to the Cosmos and sanctity – and the other one – the implementation of received knowledge, action and practicality. In essence, we are talking about a new way of thinking, which is going to determine the physical and spiritual structure of a new humanity. To summarise: sanctity, renunciation, knowledge and implementation of all the above in thoughts and emotions and its application in social structures. The coexistence of these processes cannot be mechanical, because it would stop the pendulum: it has to be a single process with gradual passage through all three stages. Every person has to become the saint, constantly increase his level of sanctity, through the comprehension of the world, unity with the Universe, and, at the same time, he has to realize himself on in emotional and practical life. Culture must always nourish civilization. The priority in the value system should always be given to sanctity and not practicality, because the Cosmos is primary and civilization is secondary.

Any civilization rests on the shoulders of the saints, not sorcerers. According to legends, people used to have an open third eye. They had access to information that can only be obtained extra-sensorily, regardless of distance and time. Later the third eye was closed. The reasons are unknown, however they are probably simple. The problem is that the acquisition of root knowledge is not permitted without observance of ethical norms, but the realization of knowledge is not directly related to ethics. At a certain point the ethical and psychological level of man lagged so far behind his energy potential that it started to threaten civilization, - therefore, the closing of the third eye was a salvation.

Regrettably the majority of the contemporary schools of spiritual and physical development cross out the two first steps – knowledge and ethics. It takes 95 percent of one's efforts and time to pass through these two steps, and there are no visible results right away. Many schools actually move in the opposite direction, and so they end up with degradation.

The evolution of a living organism is exponential: at the beginning it's a long process of accumulation of knowledge, and only after that comes realization.

For our survival at the present time, the processes of information accumulation and utilization must converge, without mutual extermination. In other words, businessmen, politicians and scientists have to become saints. Ethics have to become the first priority.

This question is especially important in bioenergetics. Attempts to use the methods of magic and sorcery for personal, mercenary interests are in conflict with the highest laws of the Universe. The result is usually tragic, but not always obvious, as the consequences appear slowly, gradually and the person sometimes cannot connect the cause and effect together. The girl that bewitched her lover has no idea that she destroys the mind, fate and bodies of her future children.

These days, tendencies developing the occult and magic abilities for a narrow personal interest is clearly defined. Nodes of the system start to behave without consideration of the entire system, this can cause the complete collapse of the system. Let's recall: the tribes with strong traditions of magic and occultism ceased developing and died out.

The world's religions are at the heart of present civilisation, in other words, they are the system that directs all human efforts to form and develop the subtle spiritual structures focussed on understanding the world. The understanding that we are all united and responsible for each other, given by religions, enabled people to feel connected with their children, parents and lovers, be aware of their responsibility for the fates of their descendants. Indirect warnings that children are accountable for the sins of their parents are given in the Bible. It's exactly the rupture of the subtle energy field structures responsible for unity with parents, children and lovers, that leads to serious illness, to the deformation of a person's fate and personality.

World religions looked after the preservation of these structures and their development. Commandments directing one to love even one's enemies have huge meaning from the bioenergetic point of view. It blocks the program of destruction of another person and, accordingly, the program of self-destruction at the energy field, subconscious level. For many centuries man has been well protected by the religious commandments of love and kindness, which safeguarded his and his children's health and, in fact, ensured the development of civilisation, even though he wasn't familiar with the laws of energy field self-regulation, and wasn't aware that his hatred may be the reason for his children's serious illness.

The system of the energy field self-regulation works automatically. Therefore, only people with well-developed subtle spiritual structures, knowing and obeying the laws of unity, laws of the Universe, could perform magic and occultism without any harm to themselves, and without risk that their children be accountable for their actions with their health, or they themselves pay by disintegration of personality. Others faced immediate disintegration of their ethical, mental and spiritual structures; they became "dark" and degenerated. Because formerly this process would take place over a longer period of time than it does now, a lot of people were under the impression that the "black magician" was the norm and not a pathology.

Presently, the spiritual incompetency of many psychics, working with complicated levels of influence, leads to their own and their close relatives' spiritual and physical disintegration. I can recall a few cases when children, relatives and even close friends and students were held responsible for the spiritual disintegration of unethical psychics. Because the energy capacity of spiritual structures is hundreds and thousands of times greater than that of physical structures, spiritual degradation remains hidden, unnoticed on the surface for a long time. When physical disintegration starts, all attempts to cure this person are blocked by the degradation of the spiritual structures; that explains the growing number of cases where medicine is helpless. Many gullibly think that if they pay a certain amount of money and attend a course they can become sorcerers or magicians. However, unlike any other science only a few can become students; these are people with relatively pure karmas, well developed spiritual structures, capable of strategic thinking, spiritual kindness and enormous self-discipline. By analysing occult and magic techniques one may notice that the most important part of them is not a set of particular methods, but the personality and qualities of the Teacher and the student. The desire of novice psychics to obtain access to higher abilities, skipping through the painful step of spiritual development, can have a pitiable result. Because a person's fate, character and the state of his physical body are determined by his energy field structure. Half-baked actions in this space can harm all of humanity.

Man's subconscious has always been securely protected. The process of entering the subconscious has been slow, accompanied by a natural culling of negative programs assisted by the ethics of society and systems of religious protection.

The psychoanalytics of different schools of psychotherapy start to assault human subconsciousness; and during recent decades this process has grown unprecedentedly. This constitutes rough invasion and the influencing of energy field structures without proper study and prognoses of long-term results of such intervention. Generally, researchers are not interested in understanding what the subconscious is and how it reacts to intrusion; they are more interested in specific and immediate results, not a deep understanding of the processes that determine the health and fate of a person and those close to him.

I would compare the lack of strategic thinking in bioenergetics and preference for tactical solutions with the actions of a driver who spends time that should be allotted to learning the driving rules on increasing the power of the engine. Very effective, but the result is risky and unpredictable.

I would like to elaborate on the methods of protection. A lack of knowledge of the fact that somebody can be influenced bio-energetically served as protection for a long time. People of «knowledge» becoming aware of this threat created hermetic schools to study bioenergetics. Ethical religious teachings, preaching kindness not only in deeds, but also in emotions and even thoughts were an excellent system of protection as well. It may seem funny, but science played a significant part in this protection by totally denying bioenergetics, the possibilities of energy and informational influence on man. Also the mechanisms of social protection from those performing magic and sorcery excessively were present.

Presently all blockages are destroyed and the brain has been exposed. The subconscious, which is in charge of all physiological and psychological processes in an organism, was being stormed as early as the last century. It started out spontaneously, but has become purposeful. Psychotherapists, psychics, sorcerers, hypnotists rudely invade the subconscious mind, focusing on the superficial effect, solving purely practical tasks. This is done with absolute ignorance of the subconscious mind, of the laws that govern its function.

My research demonstrates that the subconscious and the biofield are one and the same and any influence on biofield structures influences the subconscious, influences all systems of physiological and psychological self-regulation. Experimenters and practitioners are interested only in the depth of penetration into the subconsciousness. They would even use equipment to increase the power of influence. Bioenergetics has been converted to a science of practical influence on human beings. Nobody thinks that by healing the body we can harm the soul, that illnesses are protection, the blockage of incorrect behaviour and of misunderstanding of the surrounding world, that psychics, first of all, have to find out the cause of illness, help the person understand it and avoid these mistakes in the future. Downgrading bioenergetics to only physical aspects is a liquidation of the steps of comprehension and ethics in favour of purely practical results.

People who think that pills and magic will save them are already ill. The main safeguard against illness is the execution of the highest ethical laws.

When nature chooses physical defences – for example, increasing a dinosaur's weight or providing shells for turtles - evolution halts. Only the least protected physically and the most protected spiritually survived, only those who were prepared to change their psychological structure and behaviour according to the processes happening on Earth.

Ethics were a luxury yesterday, a necessity - today, and the only condition for survival tomorrow. People, who think only about their physical health, may follow the dinosaurs' fate. People, who are keen on magic at the expense of ethics, love and understanding the world, destroy themselves, their children and their relatives.

Today, if somebody has little energy he has to become a saint; if he has more energy he can combine his sanctity with everyday life.

Chapter 2

"The Human Being" -
A Stable Information Structure

Not so long ago there was a discussion in the medical community regarding the correctness of the term "biofield" and the number of "charlatans" was growing among the passionate supporters of this trend. Today it is difficult to find somebody who doesn't know that the dense physical body is surrounded by layers of an information-energy field, invisible to most.

Let's take a look at what a human being is from the point of view of bioenergetics. The functions and interrelations of the layers that compose this information-energy wrapper are very complicated.

Many years ago I started working with a dowsing rod and decided to discover the shape of the human energy field. Everything was great while my hand was moving parrallel to the body; I could see the boundaries of the energy field – the dowsing rod would turn 180 degrees at the edges. However, when I wanted to determine the shape of the energy field above the head I couldn't reach it while standing on the floor. I climbed on a chair raising my hand with the dowsing rod straight up, but the rod stubbornly refused to turn – hence, the boundary was even higher.

Then I decided to continue my measurements using a phantom method– I drew a human on the piece of paper and tried to measure the boundary of the field with the rod. My hand left the edge of paper, so I had to use scaling. I counted off the size of the energy field in meters, then in kilometers, but the dowsing rod was stubborn and refused to turn. Then I thought: perhaps the human field goes up to the very edge of the Universe? In response the dowsing rod turned 180 degrees. I realized that the human energy field takes up the entire Universe; above and below the boundaries of the physical body it reaches infinity.

The densities of the layers of the energy field and of the information contained therein are different. The layer of the densest energy contains the information about the state of the physical body, its organs and can be used for medical diagnosis.

The karmic structures are found in the more subtle layers and have a very complex hierarchy. The closest layers hold the information about acts, emotions, feelings and thoughts experienced by the person throughout his present life. The deeper layers contain the structures of family karma - this is information about close relatives on the paternal and maternal lines, about children.

The karma of a person, information about his behavior from previous incarnations are located on an even more subtle level. The deeper the healer penetrates the energy field of the person, the more powerful the impact he can have. This is simultaneously the strength and the weakness of the karma diagnostics. I believe that today nobody can fully penetrate a person's energy field, because any penetration means interaction, and this interaction can be safe only if the healer is a perfect human being with clean karma. An attempt to storm the subtle structures by an imperfect person can result in big problems.

Spending over two years on cleaning my karma on the daily basis, I know that there are a lot of things that I still can't change. Before every contact with the energy field of another person I check whether I am allowed to start healing this person, and if I receive a negative answer this means that my energy field contains similar violations to the ones I'm about to attempt healing. Until I have them eliminated from my own energy field I have no right to heal: my information structures can harm the patient or his structures could move to my energy field, such that my family and I would have to work off my patient's karma.

Only a perfect human being can be an ideal healer, which is unattainable in our daily life. That's why it is so important today to take another path– the path of knowledge, which allows for proper use and development of bioenergetic healing's potential, such that nobody would be hurt by improper contact with the energy field structures.

Rabindranat Tagor said that to be strong and powerful doesn't mean to excel in strength, but to help the weak to attain your heights. I thought about why so many healers couldn't pass their methods on to their students. Once and for all I decided that the most important thing is not the development of unique skills, but the ability to hand over information and teach its proper use. Before I thought that many healers didn't want to open their secrets to others in order to remain in the spotlight and receive the the maximum benefit, but later I realized that not only did they not want to, they simply couldn't.

Basically, their methods are the sum of accumulated means and techniques, which are missing the most important thing – the constant striving for understanding the world, and the systemization of received knowledge to comprehend the laws of life, of the Universe. The only exception was Jesus Christ - for him healing people was always inextricably linked to understanding the world, which he provided through parables, commandments and advice.

Despite the fact that this book is about research, often you will see such terms as "Divine", "Divine feelings", "holiness". I think no matter how well science has developed, despite the heights it has reached there will always be an area of the unknowable, unconquered by the mathematical and logical analyses of human consciousness - that area is defined by these terms.

Exploring the border areas belonging to the sphere outside logic and official science, I use terms that have a special meaning in the described system. For example, when we are talking about Divine feelings everybody will have their own perceptions of them, depending on their world-outlook and spirituality. However, the higher these feelings are on a scale of human values, the better.

The term "inanimate nature" has a collective meaning and includes, in the first place, all the gifts of the material world used by people.

Medical treatment can help thousands, while an understanding of the world can save millions. This understanding is closely related to the mechanism of penance, the effect of which I could see as a change in the karmic structures of a person.

When I realized how much the physical state is defined by the state of karmic structures in the energy field of a person, I tried to influence them in many different ways: techniques of magic, means of traditional and non-traditional medicine – I tried all sorts of things, but the results were only superficial. Later I came to a very simple conclusion: an increase in the power of influence can only traumatize the patient, it can provide a quick, visible improvement, but it is not going to change the problem fundamentally. No matter how it's wrapped, force remains force.

I realized that the most effective and safe remedy has been known to humanity for a long time – penance.

Intruding into the spiritual structures of a man with my own programs, I am guided by my own logic, my own vision of the world. Because everybody is a part of the Universe and on the subtle level everybody is connected to the Universe, it follows that, because of my imperfection, I bring something of my own into the energy field of the other person.

Any influence should be carried out only from the point of view of the whole, that is, the Universe, and this is possible when the mechanism of penance is in effect, which is directed to the soul of the Universe, that is, to God.

Why to God, why not to the entire Universe? Because, when we talk about "the Universe", in our mind we have a model of a colossal dimension, where space, time and matter are present. It is difficult for us to comprehend the Universe as a whole. Only with the rise of spirituality can individual components disappear and the feeling of Absolute Unity occurs.

When a person approaches God in his thoughts and asks for forgiveness, his soul and body undergo amazing transformations. At this moment the person recognizes his imperfection, he opens up to the Creator and receives from Him the power to change himself and come into harmony with the Universe.

There is no external influence that could replace personal aspiration.

To evaluate the state of karmic structures I use extrasensory testing, which allows me to determine the size of the measured parameter in relative terms.

The karmic structures known today can be divided into two categories: strategic and tactical. The strategic structures have a tremendous capacity, and therefore influence on them is not perceivable immediately. The state of strategic structures determines the future of the person and his descendants - that's why any attempt to misuse them or destroy them leads to a defense by the system of energy field self-regulation, often in the form of severe disease. The primary strategic parameters are "fullness of love", spirituality and soul. The tactical structures have a significantly lower capacity and they can be changed much faster. Since all parameters of the energy field of man are closely interrelated, the impact on one of them will change the values of other ones. Today we can see that the strategic reserves are quite often sacrificed for the sake of temporary improvement of a person's physical condition. There are plenty examples of such "treatments" in the life that surrounds us.

The fundamental task today is to broaden our knowledge about the world, and to strive to understand its processes and their interrelationships. It is necessary to always remember that the energy field of a human being responds instantly to any thought or emotion and that, if it is negative, the energy field responds instantly with a sharp negative reaction. The insensitivity of a person to subtle energies, to their distortions, to the inertia of the physical reaction to energy field distortions, the inability to understand the causal nature of events in one's life – all together these create misunderstanding and ignorance.

Another source of danger today is the recent increase in spiritual power in people, this means that the power of influence on others and the surrounding world has also increased. If two thousand years ago, the average value for the strength of the influence was 10 points, during the Renaissance period – 23 points, at the end of XIX century – 38 points, then now it has reached 88 points, and it continues to grow. Therefore, any negative impact has severe consequences.

The level of aggression, conscious and subconscious, plays an important role among the parameters of the tactical structures. Conscious aggression we can feel right away and react to it; the danger of subconscious aggression is that it's impossible to control it from the conscious mind. However, our energy field reacts to it instantly with returned aggression, and, since the power of influence keeps rising, we are constantly involved in invisible battles, without even knowing about it - we only face the consequences.

Subconscious aggression – this parameter must have a negative value in the system of the parameters that comprise the energy field of a human being, and the higher its absolute value, the better it is. This is a foundation for genuine kindness in a person and is also important for protection against foreign aggression.

A very important characteristic of the biofield is the level of connection to the Cosmos. Its value depends significantly on the ethics of the person and his ancestors. The greatest violation, which destroys these structures, is killing love.

The feeling of love is multifaceted and, first of all, it has to be directed to God and the Universe, thanks to which we obtain unity with the Universe and, accordingly, unity with our parents, children and loved ones. No living or inanimate creature should not be deprived of our love. When we will be able to understand this and start to work in this direction daily and hourly, truthfully evaluating ourselves, our actions, feelings, thoughts our lives will become much more enjoyable.

The mechanism of karma regulates the unity and relationship of a human being with the Universe. The better we know this mechanism, the shorter our path to overcoming our problems will be. Generally speaking, humanity has all the necessary information about the laws of interaction in the world, concisely and brilliantly stated in religious commandments. However, we are, like doubting Thomas, constantly butting our heads against the same obstacles, destroying the world and ourselves and stubbornly refusing to make the right conclusions. Today we have the opportunity to "probe" the fairness of the laws expressed in the commandments with our own hands, to connect science and religion, to evaluate in the language of numbers, the state to which we have brought the world and to try to find our way to World Harmony.

Chapter 3

Extrasensory Testing

Exploring the human biofield I came to the conclusion that the energy field structures and the physical body exist as two opposites, mutually influencing each other. The speed of transition of the energy field structures into the physical body and the reverse can be different.

My experience in healing different illnesses has shown that treatment is much more effective if the influence is aimed not at a sick organ, not even at the entire organism, but at the cause of the illness. No matter how much effort we put into the treatment of a particular illness, if the cause is not eliminated it will continue to nourish this illness, and, in practice, the illness can even move from one organ to another. An illness is not like an avalanche that can be removed by clearing a small area, an illness is like water running out of a tap, so first we must close the tap, eliminating the cause of the illness.

Analyzing the deformations of the energy field structures that appear in the energy field of a human being, I discovered that many illnesses begin at the energy field level, often many years before they manifest on the physical level. The cause of energy field deformation is the discrepancy between the characteristics of the energy field of the person and the information field of the Earth and the Universe. Thoughts, emotions or behavior, which are in conflict with the harmony of the Universe, lead to deformations of energy field structures. Consequently, the elimination of the causes of these deformations is the way to the person's recovery.

At the beginning, I believed that there should be about five to seven of these structures reflecting energy field deformations. However, as my research progressed, it became clear that there are a huge number of them. Every negative action, thought or emotion creates "adhesions" in the layers of the person's energy field, and their elimination harmonizes the energy field structures and the physical condition of this person. After analyzing hundreds of cases, I realized that illness, injury, life troubles, the disintegration of personality, character or mind – these are all different versions of redemption, the process of eliminating the causes of energy field deformation and its harmonization. I felt that the physical body is not the only element of the united system of organs, mutually influencing each other. Spiritual structures, mind, fate and character are also elements of this system. Influence on any of the mentioned parameters automatically initiates changes in the rest, therefore, for example, a rise in spirituality improves the mind, destiny and health - simultaneously improves all aspects of the person's life. Any problems in a person's life – misfortune, physical and mental disease, injuries – these all result from the system of energy field self-regulation, the necessary intervention blocking the start of spiritual structure decay – the main strategic structures responsible for the survival of the person and of his descendants.

While working and influencing the information-energy complex of a human being it is crucial for me to assess the results of this influence, otherwise while helping the person's body I could destroy important karmic structures. Bioenergetic influence is much stronger than any medication, but, also, much more dangerous, therefore it's necessary to have a system for keeping records while I am working. Thus gradually the main principles and elements of the system of extrasensory testing were developed, allowing the estimation of parameters and to monitor the results of impact on the energy field structures.

Analyzing the correlation between the main parameters of the system of self-regulation, I began to understand the laws of organism development more deeply, I discovered karmic structures that protect people from misfortunes and injuries, and also discovered structures of success and luck, which our organism constantly renews and reproduces. The destruction of these structures happens when people reject God, their parents, their children and loved ones. There are particular structures in the energy field responsible for a person's ability to love and their deformation leads to the most serious illnesses, including cancer.

Since the physical body together with karmic structures comprise a single process (because every object is simultaneously a process), it is possible to test it, forecast its future state and, accordingly, carry out early diagnosis, evaluating any influence on a person. The method allows for testing groups of people, social programs and even entire countries, to provide long-term forecasts, to estimate behavior and destiny of living and inanimate objects. In today's world, when the consequences of any catastrophe are becoming more and more severe, the development of this method of early discovery of critical situations, for individuals, groups, organizations and even industrial facilities is not only justified, but necessary for survival.

The method of extrasensory testing allows us to analyze not only the physical parameters of an object, but also its energy field structure. Since future events of the material world originate in the energy field structures, life situations at the physical level are the realization of existing programs at the energy field level. Any event that takes place in the Universe is not a chaotic interaction of different objects, but the implementation of particular programs, which are encoded in the information-energy field of the Universe. It is a series of events, proceeding from information into energy structures being realized on the physical level. The mechanism of karma is a reflection of the principle of unity of man and the Universe.

Based on examples of treatments for different illnesses, analysis of my patients difficult life situations, as well as testing different programs and objects, I will try, not only to uncover the potential of the method of extrasensory testing, but also to pass on the information accumulated during my work about our major mistakes - the causes that lead to a person's inability to live in harmony with the Universe, and, as a result, suffer sickness, sorrow, suffering and misfortune.

The First Cause

Many processes that are taking place in our lives today are aimed at removing the blockages between a person's consciousness and his subconscious. Everything that gets into the subconscious becomes a guide to action.

If about 100 - 150 years ago only art, philosophy and some esoteric schools were engaged in storming the subconscious mind, then today medical science has joined in the fray.

The logic of the human mind is focused on the survival of the physical body, while the logic of subconscious mind – at maintaining and development of spiritual structures, therefore, attempts to mechanically align them in many cases can lead to the destruction of one of them.

Presently, the human subconscious absorbs energy "dirt" at an incredible speed - not only because so many want to penetrate it, but also because nowadays confused people have become too trusting. It's sufficient to express even one percent of doubt about received information – and our subconscious mind will already be protected from it.

Negative feelings and emotions that have reached the subconscious are not controlled by the person any more, and since physical health is closely connected to the subconscious, the consequences can be very complicated.

A male patient had a consultation with me, complaining about constant headaches. I found the reason for his illness. Ten years before our meeting he strongly resented his wife, with cause. After I described everything to him he asked me in astonishment-

"Everything is correct, but how did you guess? "

"I have no right to guess. I examine the causes of the disease and I can see them. Resentment is one of the most common violations of the laws of the Universe, causing different troubles for the offended person, as well as for the offender."

I spoke with the mother of a ten-year old girl. She complained that her daughter's classmates don't want to be friends with her.

"Can you tell me these girls names?" – after testing I could see that all of the girls mentioned were very negative towards this woman's daughter.

"In 1974 you hurt the feelings of a woman" I explain to the mother. "This resentment formed a deformation in your energy field structure, which migrated into your daughter's energy field, and this program is aimed against women. Those girls sense it and don't want to be friends with your daughter."

After correcting the mother's energy field structures I could see the changes in these girls' attitude towards her daughter. The next day the classmates became friends with her. The mother had to carry on the correction of the energy field structures herself, even though she was not a psychic and has the energy level of an average person, but precise focus on the spots of the energy field requiring correction and my help – my help in reaching a spiritual contact with the Universe will bring the desired result.

Once I was helping a young man's grandmother. Her main violation was a massive resentment towards her mother. During difficult life circumstances her mother offended her somehow. Perhaps, she couldn't do anything differently, but her daughter had been holding the resentment for many years. Her son's and grandson's health and destiny were not fortunate. Since on the energy field level parents and children experience a very tight union, if a child resents his parents, or the parent resents a child, this can rupture or deform the most subtle structures which are responsible for normal, kind relationships between people. The grandmother resented her mother, the deformation of her energy field structures was transferred to her son, and son was married five or six times. He divorced every time, maintaining good relationships with his ex-wives, however, they couldn't maintain the families. Her grandson has the same problem, constant problems in his personal life. He is a wonderful, kind person, meets remarkable girls, but he can't create a stable family.

Studies of karmic structures vividly demonstrate the biblical commandment at the energy level: *"Honor your father and your mother, that your days may be prolonged on the earth..."*

The attitude towards the mother and father should always be respectful. The set of laws and regulations that existed in all ages of society, protected the most subtle structures of the human energy field from destruction. Today we've lost all of this.

An interesting story happened not long ago. A woman called me, her husband had an urgent long-term business trip coming, but he suffered from severe radiculitis. I checked his condition from a distance and it was quite poor.

Not long before he had a preinfarction angina and now strong lower back pain. He was preparing to go see a doctor to help him eliminate the pain, but it's a good thing that he didn't make it, because then he would have had problems with his heart. This still young man already had karmic deformations – mostly because of a strong feeling of resentment inherited from his mother and father. He would take offence subconsciously, often without even being aware of it. During the last few years any conflict resulted in his unintentionally attacking people on the energy field level – he would take offence and, consequently, receive a responding blow. That began to have a negative impact on his physical condition, and, first of all, on his heart. He is a kind, sympathetic person; his spiritual and emotional parameters were quite high, which worked as the best protection for him, so his main punishment went onto his body and he became sick. Through his physical suffering he was saving his soul. The fact that he got severe back-pain saved him from a heart attack, because the powerful deformation in his energy field had to result in a serious physical illness, functional or organic. If he were to receive a massage or painkiller, he could have had problems with his heart. I received this information through testing his energy field structures at a distance.

We had to clear his karma, remove the main cause of the disease. I called him every hour and explained the violations committed by his parents. The level of his subtle energy, which had been catastrophically low, began to rise slowly. The most important thing for me was to normalize his main parameters, to clear his energy field from karmic structures. Not to remove the physical pain, but to eliminate the source, because simple elimination of physical pain could have come at a high cost. The harmonization of karmic structures is a method that doesn't provide instant results. I might not have had enough time to heal him before he left for his trip, but I was blocking the cause of the illness. I called him a few times until midnight.

Then I checked him in the morning – and again there was an overall drop in the energy level and the same energy field deformation. The reason for this was that he was offended with me. In the evening he tried to get up, but he fell down and lost consciousness from the pain. He wasn't prepared for my method of healing, he believed that after psychic influence the result should come instantly. I explained that he shouldn't be offended, he had been violating the highest laws for so many years that it couldn't be fixed in a few hours. I continued the influence. The next evening his pain was gone and he left for his business trip.

However, a few days later his wife called me asking to check their daughter. The girl had lost consciousness in school and doctors couldn't figure out what was wrong with her. It turned out that it was her father's fault. The girl's condition worsened significantly because her dad took offence at me again; but because my karma is relatively clear his offence came back to him, and the impact fell on his child.

Formerly, when there were saints, who respected the highest laws, any person who would get offended at them, received punishment immediately. This worked as a preventative instrument, people understood that they couldn't take offence – they could really see and feel it. These days we all have negative karma, so any resentment "falls through" into the energy field and there is no immediate punishment – we die slowly. A lack of understanding and insensitivity don't allow us to see the real processes.

My next patient told me that she got divorced from her husband and she believes that it was his mother's fault. His mother did everything to try and make them fall apart, although at first glance, it looked like she treated her daughter in law well. I began to investigate the reason for this kind of behavior from his mother and found that even before her child was born she hated her husband, resented him and she kept these feelings for a long time. She set her mind on separating with her husband. Negative feelings formed an information block, which remained in her subconscious mind, even though she'd forgot about this a long time ago living a normal life with her husband. However, her mindset remained in her energy field and started to destroy, not her own relationship, but her son's relationship. The program destroying the relationship between people influenced her beloved person - her son and demolished his destiny and relationship with his wife. On the surface, the mother can explain to herself that she just didn't like her daughter-in-law, but in reality, it was the mechanism of the preservation of evil: once committed, evil does not disappear – it remains in the subconscious and, sooner or later, spills out, and often affects those closest to us, the ones we love the most.

A young woman came to me for a consultation, asking to heal her child from a skin rash. I found the reason, explained what happened and when, what the person she was upset with looked like, but she couldn't remember. I began to heal her child, because I could see the energy field distortions.

After a little while the woman told me that her child got worse and rash spread. I analyzed the cause and discovered that at the beginning I had only seen the superficial layer, that there was more than one cause. This woman had lost her first child. The reason for her first child's death and the second child's severe rash was that she strongly resented her husband. After correction her child felt a little bit better, but the energy field deformations wouldn't go away completely.

"You continue to be angry with your husband," I explain to the woman.

"But he is the one to blame, he hurt me!"

I explained to her that he could not be at fault. Relationships between people are determined by encodings in their energy fields. Every person's energy field has a collection of programs that determine his interaction with the world and people. Feelings of love, anger, resentment, experienced by those around you, strictly correspond to what lies in your karma. So that's why there are people who are constantly bullied, there are people who get hurt, there are people who are jealous and so on. A person's energy field contains programs responsible for his attitude towards people and people's attitude towards him. When there is something unpleasant done to us, it's not permitted to respond with the same action. We can only resist on the physical level, but on the energy field, spiritual level we must retain humility, gentleness, and love towards people. We have to remember that any problem is the result of our imperfection, that, when taken the right way, it removes negative karma, saves us from diseases and improves our children's health and destiny.

Irritability with other people, anger – these are all attempts of energy attacks not only at a particular person, but at the entire Universe, leading to deformations of the energy field structures. *"Bless them that curse you, do good to them that hate you and pray for those who persecute you..."* This is the most reliable protection against misfortune, diseases and from what we call the "evil eye".

My assistant wanted to help her cousin. I explained to her what kind of violations her cousin's mother committed and the assistant went to church. Suddenly she found herself not feeling well there. When I checked her energy field - it completely "fell apart". One of the reasons was that she herself had resented her cousin's mother, and without realizing it, without releasing this feeling she came to the icon asking for forgiveness on this relative's behalf. Even a subconscious resentment or wishing of evil within the scope of the church's, the icon's energy field, which is aimed at love and people's unity, can amplify and distort the person's energy field structures.

During a consultation, a woman asked me to test, at a distance, the room where she worked, as recently, somehow, she didn't want to be there. I checked the energy structure of the premise and found three powerful negative zones, each of which had a different "person at fault". The most dangerous and unpleasant one was a zone about a meter in radius that was created by a male, whose age and appearance I described to her. The woman was confused because the described co-worker was a very gentle and polite person, treated her wonderfully and the idea of him creating a program of destruction and hatred that appeared in her room seemed simply impossible.

Further investigation showed that she was right and wrong at the same time, as the co-worker's program of destruction of women and hatred towards them worked on the subconsciousness level. Generally this is the case when these program creators are either ancestors or these violations were committed by this person in past incarnations. In this case, the program was initiated by the co-worker's grandmother, who didn't want to be pregnant and wished that her baby girl would die.

This program was so strong that it continued to live for several following generations. The completely unaware successor of this program subconsciously destroyed women. This also affected his personal life. His first wife said that occasionally she would experience some strange feeling towards him and without understanding or being aware of what she was doing, she even rushed at him with a knife. So they separated. His relationship with his second wife was much better, but after 5 years of living together she died in an accident.

After examining the energy field structures of these two women, I realized that both of these cases had the same reason: an autonomous program against women that existed in the energy field of this man. In addition, this program would work more intensely the more attached he was to a woman. He didn't have children, boys had no chance of being born as they would carry their dad's program and unintentionally destroy a lot of women, and girls would be lacking vitality.

My patient wanted to help her co-worker and she knew that I could correct the person's energy field using drawing (that is to influence person's subconsciousness through drawing) so she asked me to step in. I eliminated this program from the energy field of this person at a distance. This is one of the magic tricks that I usually don't use. I don't know why I changed my principles and agreed, as only spiritual changes and comprehension can heal somebody, but here there was an element of magic. Perhaps, I was anxious to help this lady as soon as I could, and, definitely, make an impression. It was a very comforting feeling to be the master of somebody's fate. Our meeting came to the end and I was very pleased.

However, in about four hours I had the feeling of acute danger. I was looking for the reasons and realized what had happened. The problem was that the program of destruction can be neutralized only through penance, and if you just take it out of the energy field of a person it continues to exist somewhere else. I had to find where this program had gone. It turned out that it was in my energy field. Then I realized why sorcerers remove illnesses in water, earth, plants, and different objects – otherwise this program will act against those who had taken it out. I tried to find this program in my own energy field structures, but couldn't find it there, I did, however, find it in my son's energy field. He was supposed to inherit the karma of the person I just saved, he would have to destroy women that he loved. I couldn't leave this program in my son's energy field, but also I felt sorry for this man. I managed to neutralize about sixty percent of the program, but the rest I had to return to the owner, because at that point he had already done enough to support the program with his own actions towards women. The idea of transferring illness into water is incorrect as well, but we will talk about that later.

A great number of illnesses are related to the fact that people don't know how dangerous it is to have negative emotions during periods of spiritual elevation, happiness, love, when a person's energy level increases dramatically.

Once a woman approached me asking for help, her child suffered enuresis. I found the cause of the illness and shared it with the mother:

"You resented or wished evil upon somebody during the year of (such and such) ."

The woman couldn't remember. I clarified:

"It was in February, approximately the 11th-12th."

"It was my wedding day!"

"What happened at your wedding?"

The woman couldn't recall any strong negative emotions or actions related to her wedding. Nevertheless, at the energy plane I could see a very powerful resentment at the husband's relative.

"Is it possible that you got into arguments with your mother-in-law?"

The woman could hardly remember that, indeed, her mother-in-law said something wrong, but she couldn't remember any strong negative feeling about it, which she would retain in her memory.

I began to understand what had happened.

"On your wedding day you were in an exalted state of mind, the level of your subtle energy was high, and, as a result, even a minor unintentionally offence at your mother-in-law that, caused great harm to this woman. This resentment returned back to you and formed enuresis for your child.

Enuresis – this is not a disease, this is the first sign of serious troubles with the child's spiritual structures, this is a time bomb, and will not necessary appear as a disease, the child might have an unhappy fate or his emotional and mental structures can be distorted.

Any feeling of resentment, which has gone deep inside or which a person cannot handle during a long period of time, carries great danger. Intuitively people always try to throw off, defuse the feeling of resentment, and don't allow it to accumulate. Crying, smashing dishes and swearing worked perfectly for this purpose. If resentment is experienced during a long period of time it becomes much more dangerous and affects not only the offender and the offended, but also their children. Healthy people usually don't allow themselves to stay upset for a long time. There is a holiday in Judaism and Christianity (Forgiveness Sunday – for Orthodox Christians), on this day a person asks for forgiveness for all his wrong feelings inflicted on others, voluntarily or involuntarily. If it's done sincerely, then it triggers the mechanism of penance and the purification of the subconscious follows.

I am afraid that we have a very vague understanding of the meaning of penance.

Studying the religions of the world I was interested in the term repentance. This is, first of all, not the fruitless remorse, self-torture or regrets of the past. By experiencing these emotions a person can only create harm for himself. Repentance means to put all efforts on changing oneself, and to never again repeat the same mistakes. Repentance is a process, the meaning of which is to direct the burst of energy occurring when **realizing wrongdoing,** towards development. The disconnection of the chain of cause and effect occurs as a result of repentance, where one act no longer leads to another one. The mechanism of transmission of energy field information, such as accumulation and activation of negative programs and their implementation through emotions and actions, can be stopped.

In Judaism, it is considered that the repentant, and in Christianity – the thief on the cross, can turn out to be higher than a saint, because they need to spend much more effort on repentance than any person with a pure karma to live all life in holiness. A person with a pure family and personal karma often requires much less effort to achieve much greater results, than the person with a loaded karma – even if it's just to behave in a moral way. Therefore, all religions of the world clearly articulate the thesis that personal aspiration of man for the Divine is much more significant than the abilities given to him by nature.

The mechanism of repentance is inseparably connected to a correct vision of the world: to be able to understand when a law has been violated, one must first know the law.

Initially, I assumed that repentance breaks only programs formed by negative emotions, such as hatred, resentment or wishing of evil, but now I see that it has a much greater potential, and most importantly – it's a powerful change and harmonization of the energy field structures.

On the subtle, spiritual level every person is in contact with the Divine, as every cell of an organism connects with the entire organism. It is impossible to interrupt this contact no matter how bad the karma and no matter how the person behaves.

The energy field structures of every person contain information about the violations of the highest laws by his ancestry and himself in previous incarnations. The more serious the violation the more subtle the level where this information is stored. It becomes easier to understand the existence of two opposite theses - original sin and the original purity of man - if we remember the different levels of the energy field structures.

Aspiration for the Unknowable, for the Divine through love and penance permits access to more subtle levels, is the spiritual elevation of man and the purification of karma. Man is imperfect on the outside, but inside he is similar to God, as he is created "in the image and likeness of" God. By approaching Him we clean ourselves.

The unity of everything surrounding us manifests in most unexpected ways.

One day my acquaintance called complaining that her dog was dying – it ate some sort of poison and nobody knew whether it would survive. I checked the dog's energy field from a distance, and found black spots in the stomach and head areas – the poison had affected the brain. The dog was motionless.

"Is it possible to influence poison energetically?"

"Yes, we can" – I started to neutralize the poison from a distance in the dog's body and tested what kind of medicine could be given.

"You can dissolve aspirin in a glass of water and let your dog drink it."
- I suggested to my acquaintance over the phone.

The black spot began to change in half an hour – it became gray and reduced in size. Slowly the dog started to feel better. Nevertheless it was important for me to know why the dog had eaten the poison in the first place. I continued to examine and discovered that the reason for the incident with the dog lay in the owner's behavior, in her violation of the highest laws of the Universe some time ago.

I talked to a young woman. She was in a car accident and had a concussion as a result, and now her finger was numb. I searched for the reason for the accident, analyzed the consequences and explained to this woman the relationship between her behavior and the accident.

"And what about my health?" she asked.

When an unprepared person comes for my consultation, he or she expects that I am going to do magic with my hands and have difficulty understanding my explanations, with understanding immediately that this influence is much stronger. Sometimes patients can even start resenting me and, unfortunately, this doesn't pass without consequences for them.

A few days later this woman had a great improvement in her condition, but when she came to see me again, I found a distortion in her energy field. It was because of her original lack of confidence in my information and the automatic energy attack directed at me. I explained it to the woman.

"That is impossible!"

"Look, I describe the situation: ten minutes after you left you felt dissatisfaction. As your karma is not very clear, your parents' karmic violations got on board as well and it became a real attack on me. Have you had any problems recently?"

"Yes, my dog was almost hit by a car."

I drew the energy field structures of the woman and her dog. They are identical. Pets are very dependent on their owner's ethics, and their illnesses and traumas, in most cases, are caused by their owners. The energy field of the dog was clear before, but after her visit to me distortions appeared in the area of its head and front and back legs.

"Here's the dog's paw injury," I showed the woman on the picture. "Whose fault is this? The owner. What did she do? She wished me wrong. When you left you were irritated for fifteen minutes," I explain in detail. "but, because I am innocent, your resentment "fled" to your dog. You are lucky that it wasn't to your husband or son."

I corrected the woman's energy field, and as a result her dog's condition started to improve, but there still was a distortion in the back paw area because the woman didn't yet agree with all of the received information. In a while the dog's energy field completely leveled out.

Our relatives and even our pets depend on us, and if we violate the laws of ethics they may be punished along with us.

Recently I receive a lot of phone calls from my acquaintances regarding different medical issues. One of them had bronchitis for twenty days already, doctors had tried different medications, but the disease was just getting worse.

"A month ago you resented your wife."

"She was very much at fault, I almost hit her, even."

"Remember: you can't stay offended with your close relatives for a long period of time, and even more importantly, it's forbidden to allow it to get inside. This is the same as resenting the Universe."

In two days my acquaintance called to say that his bronchitis was completely gone. A consultation that opened the cause for the disease saved him from long-term medical treatment; what's more the better the treatment he would receive the worse it would have turned out for him, because the cause for the illness would have continued to exist.

In these cases using qigong exercises and diet therapy are quite acceptable, as they can influence the person's mind and subconscious demolishing the programs of disintegration created by resentment. However, these means have no control over one's conscious mind and thus provide only partial healing, they won't relieve the person from the reoccurrence of similar situations.

Now let's imagine that the described situation developed a little bit differently: in one-two months the person was cured with the help of modern medicine, but the reason for bronchitis – resentment - remained as a package of programs in his subconscious. If around this time or a few months later his wife would give birth to a child then the program of resentment and destroying people, received from his father, would enter the child's energy field. This child, growing up, would carry a time bomb inside, and even insignificant resentment towards some close relative could initiate this mechanism. Tuberculosis, heart attack, or tumors of the lung, stomach, or esophagus could develop to block this program.

Nowadays people's incorrect behavior is not blocked by a corresponding worldview, by a high level of ethics, culture or by obeying the commandments in the Bible, for example, therefore, everybody carries these "bombs" in their energy fields and they explode more and more often. This explains the outbursts of cardiovascular diseases and cancer during recent decades. Since medicine is not aware of this mechanism, doctors are trying to find an explanation in the deterioration of the environment, poor-quality food or frequent stress.

Even this story shows - if the entire arsenal of modern medicine is directed at only eliminating the consequences, as usual, it will be impossible to prevent those "Chernobyls" which are just waiting to assault our health.

The logic of the conscious mind and the logic of life and the development of the Universe, often don't correspond, unfortunately. The conscious mind and the lowest level of the subconscious are contrary to the harmonization of the world, and almost every story described in this book confirms this.

A young man came to see me for the second time. During our first session I explained that his inner aggression towards women was the cause of his wife's infertility. As a result of the correction we managed to reduce his aggression, but at the second meeting I could see that his negative programs were very active again.

"Your program of destruction towards your wife is on again. What could be the reason for this?"

"Recently I saw my first wife and we got into an argument again."

"You have to let go of all complaints and resentments towards your first wife, forgive her and leave all negative emotions related to her behind."

"I have forgiven her for everything, but several of her actions still bother me."

"Resentment, as hatred or jealousy, is one of the forms of human destruction, it is an energy attack. If you can't understand that and aren't able to balance your feelings towards your first wife, I won't be able to help you. The program of destruction of your wife is not a reaction to the names – Masha or Luba – but to a woman who you see as your wife. Your first wife energetically is not your wife any more, thus an activation of complaints and resentment towards her destroys your second wife. You have to forgive your enemy if you want to avoid killing each other.

If you aren't be able to overcome this than all of your hatred towards your first wife will be automatically turned on even at the smallest disagreement with your second wife. The programs of destruction, if you don't block them completely, can reappear in the energy fields of your children and will cause their illnesses or can continue to lengthen your wife's infertility. Resenting your first wife, you are already killing your future children. Humility, which is described in Christianity, is not slavery, as it was interpreted for a long time, but a mechanism for spiritual growth. Harmony with the Universe on a subtle level can be achieved through inner humility."

Recently a man had a consultation with me, whose family was on the verge of separation. However, he couldn't give a reason for it, because he had a good relationship with his wife. It turned out that the cause of the problem was his mother. She didn't like his first wife and did everything possible to separate them. So they did separate. The second daughter-in-law was liked very much by his mother, but the program of destruction of her son's Divine feelings got turned on automatically in her subconscious mind and against the beloved daughter-in-law. Being unaware of this, his mother constantly programmed her son and daughter-in-law to ruin their best feelings for each other and to separate.

A person's consciousness is like a small wheel, which one can rotate in any direction with little effort. The subconscious is a huge, heavy wheel that's difficult to get moving and even harder to stop it. Our ancestry spun the wheel of the subconscious by aspiring to God, love and kindness. The last three centuries we have been living off the momentum of this movement and putting in little effort to maintain it. Hence only our constant conscious aspiration for world harmony and towards God can save us now. Today personal aspiration of every individual in particular will determine the degree of his protection against misfortune.

Not long ago my acquaintance called:

"I got into an argument with my friend and now I am choking with resentment. Many times I asked for forgiveness for feeling offended, but nothing helps."

"It doesn't help because you should ask for forgiveness not only for yourself, but also for your friend, for her feeling resentful towards you. You should ask that she would be forgiven as well."

The woman hesitated:

"But it was mostly her fault, I didn't harm her."

I took a pause to help her understand my thoughts and explain:

"We always offend somebody subconsciously first, who later offends us by their behavior. In your past life you offended women and by doing this you created a mechanism of resentment, which works automatically on your subconscious level. On top of this, your father hurt your mother's feelings during her first few months of pregnancy, consequently resentment in your subconscious can be activated even by the slightest cause, which your conscious mind wouldn't even register.

Therefore, if somebody offends you, first of all, you have to ask for forgiveness for offending this person first. That will block the karmic structures of your parents and your past lives, which created this situation in the first place. After that you have to apologize for the fact that you were not able to forgive the other person, and experienced resentment towards him. Only after that you can ask for forgiveness for the offender, for him resenting you or offending you. Every time you feel resentment you should try internally to justify the person's behavior and after that – to forgive. Only with this behavior you can block the karmic structures of destruction and disintegration; this will help to preserve your own and your children's health."

All of the above applies to the person's inner state; the external reaction can be different. The most important thing is that this mechanism should work in your soul.

The Second Cause

Once I asked my patient:

"What do you think is the worst crime man can commit in his life?"

"The murder of another person."

"Actually, there is a greater crime that exists - this is the killing of love, because before you kill somebody, first you have to kill the love inside you towards this person. Killing the feeling of love is the basis for many crimes and misfortunes.

There was a couple from a village at my consultation. Their fifteen year old son, after watching a famous comedian perform on TV and laughing, went into the hall ... and hung himself. The parents couldn't comprehend how this could happen. I searched for the cause, analyzed what happened to this boy. It turned out that the mother had had a friend who loved her deeply, but she didn't feel the same way and deliberately destroyed his love. He couldn't take it anymore, threw himself under a train and died. What happened? The mother killed the love and life in a loving man. According to the law of karma, she received this powerful program of destruction of love back. For many years this package was in her energy field, but it realized itself in her son's energy field, activating itself at a certain moment when he was fifteen.

There are hundreds of different programs in the energy field structure of a person, which are formed by actions, thoughts, emotions not only of an individual, but also by his relatives.

There is an expression in Eastern philosophy: "There are no people, only ideas." The reason for unmotivated crimes, murder (including suicides) often lies in the programs of destruction and self-destruction created by the criminal's ancestors and their victims, hidden in the subconscious until a certain time. Programs not only remain in the energy fields for decades, but also accumulate power, gaining energy from similar violations by the person's children and grandchildren, if they are not blocked by ethical norms and aspiration for the Divine.

A woman came for a consultation. She was infertile. She had already visited a few psychics, but there had been no result. I explained to her the cause of the problem:

"Four times you had suicidal thoughts, you initiated inside yourself the program that ruins love and life. This program is very strong, and your organism must stop it. By suppressing love in yourself, suppressing the feeling that connects you to everybody, you harm not only yourself, but also others.

The woman interrupted me:

"Never mind about other people, I just want to know what is happening with me in particular"

I continued explaining patiently:

"Now you reject all people, for your benefit, now you're rejecting love once again. While you retain this feeling you are going to have problems, and not only with infertility.

"Tell me specifically, will I get better? What can you guarantee?"

I am overworking, at the edge of my potential. I get tired from any tactless question.

"I can't guarantee anything, because too many things depend on you."

The woman got up and left silently. I checked her emotions: the positive thing is that she didn't get offended and didn't cause even more damage to herself.

There was a young twenty year old girl in my office. Usually I don't ask what brought them to me, I sense it myself. The girls' physical state was quite good, but her spiritual structures were seriously deformed, though it hadn't reflected on her health yet.

"Generally speaking, you are in pretty good health. A small tachycardia, but overall nothing serious."

She stared at me with a dull, indifferent glance.

"I have diabetes."

Before I would have been shocked by the supposedly incorrect diagnosis. A person is seriously ill and I say that she should be in perfect health. However, now, after studying the causes for the disease, I know that her diabetes is, first of all, the defensive reaction of her organism. Her organism must stop the programs of destruction of other people, which appeared in it. The more dangerous and powerful the program of destruction, the more effective and reliable the blocking has to be, meaning the disease.

I examined the reason for the diabetes: when she was fourteen she was in love with a young man, the love was very strong, but they broke up. They broke up because their information fields were incompatible. In a physical world this can manifest in different ways. As a result the girl began hating this young man. She killed her love, regretted the break up and directed powerful ill wishes in his direction. These feelings caused the development of diabetes, because one of the most important laws of the Universe was violated and her connection with the Cosmos was interrupted. Rejection of the highest feelings greatly distorts energy field structures and often appears on the physical level as an incurable disease.

A disease can perform different functions. The first function – warning, the second – the suspension of activity that interferes with a person's correct development, and the third – the elimination of mechanisms that allow one to spread negative information. We must always remember that we are the cells of a united organism called "humanity", which in turn is part of a united system – the Universe. All the basic commandments of world religions are encrypted concepts of world order and the rules of our relationship with it. Now we are given the opportunity to expand our vision of the world and to see what used to be available only to the Great Initiates.

My next patient had no complaints about her health, but she couldn't cope with the adversity in her personal life. She loved a man. She was loved by him as well, but there were always difficulties and she couldn't figure out what was going on. It seemed as if destiny would constantly pull them apart.

I tested the situation looking for who there was to blame. The reason was quite remote, in the events of the early 20s. Her grandmother with her behavior rejected love as a Divine feeling; her actions were intended to kill love. At the beginning of 20's her grandmother got married for convenience, to save her belongings. The family was dispossessed anyway and the grandmother left her husband without any regrets. She confessed to her granddaughter that she never loved her husband. But he loved her deeply and struggled for quite a while. The young woman told me this story in tears and she added that their relationship with Peter is in complete discord now as well.

"What was your grandmother's husband name?"

The woman looked at me astonished and said:

"Peter!"

I studied the energy field structure and could conduct a medical diagnosis. The main problem of the woman, who came to see me, is a gynecological disease.

"Eight years ago a man loved you"

"Yes" – she nodded.

"Did you like him?"

"No."

"He was pining away because of you, and you killed love in him. Instead of breaking up gently, showing that this is not your fault, you did it quite harshly."

"Yes, I didn't treat him the way I would today."

"What you've done is the reason for your diseases today. Did you have any other problems? Did you have a pregnancy interruption?"

"Two times: I wanted to have kids, but it didn't happen."

"You were supposed to have boys."

"Really? And what happened?"

"Because you killed love in a man, in this case the boys were lacking vitality. Do you have kids now?"

"A daughter."

"Did you try to have more kids?"

"I got in a car accident, I had an injury in the hip area, pelvic bones were fractured, so I can't give birth anymore."

"Do you understand that your injury wasn't an accident?"

""Now I do."

Sometimes it is difficult to believe how much our actions affect our physical state, but every new case provides irrefutable proof that disease goes away as soon as the right cause for the disease is detected.

Once the host of a house I was visiting showed me a video of his niece's wedding, which was a year ago. The wedding was stunning: a young and beautiful bride, happy groom, cheerful relatives. Looking at the bride I completely automatically tested her and found that there were serious problems awaiting this family.

"Can you invite your niece over immediately?" I asked the host. "She requires some treatment, because she might have great difficulties with childbirth."

"Three months ago she gave birth to a lifeless child."

"She should come anyway. This is just the beginning."

I completed a more in-depth diagnostic and found the deformations in the girl's energy field, which pertain to the the most serious violations of the highest laws. There was a classic case of so-called dying family.

"Do you know that there is damnation on the maternal side of your family?"

"Yes, a fortune-teller told us about that."

"Did she tell you the reason?"

"No, usually they don't know."

"Call all your relatives from your mother's side urgently. There is only one reason in your family for all the deaths of children, incurable diseases and severe misery."

The next day all of the relatives were in front of me. I described to them what was happening to all of them.

"You grandfather during his wife's pregnancy committed a violation and now all of his descendants are held responsible for it. He rejected the child during the fifth month of his wife pregnancy.

Why is the punishment so severe? During the fifth month a child is absolutely united with God dand the Universe. To maintain a normal life people must occasionally come in contact with the Universe, thus they use the memories from the fifth month after conception encoded in their energy fields. If the father or mother rejected the child during this time, and this can happen subconsciously, in a big quarrel for example, then the child inherits not only the program of destroying his children, but also the Universe. The cell carries the program of destruction of the organism, and the organism responds to it accordingly. The only way to block this program is through aspiration to God and by being filled with love. If a person fails to do this, the collapse of his family is inevitable.

I could see how the people in front of me turned to God in their thoughts, how the structures of damnation left their energy fields. And once again I am convinced, that the best way to heal somebody is, first of all, through understanding.

Our children have energy potential that is ten times higher compared to that of our ancetors' children, a few generations ago. Nevertheless we pay too little attention to our children's spiritual development; we focus them primarily on their professional activities, taking care of the future material wealth of our descendants.

Not long ago one of my acquaintances, a gifted psychic, had a problem – her dog got paralyzed, it couldn't feel its back legs. She asked me to help her find the cause. I was amazed at what I saw, she was pregnant on the third month and her child, correctly speaking – fetus, started to feel jealous of his mother's affection towards the dog and initiated the program destroying the animal. I examined the reasons for such high aggression in her child. The mother prayed for him and the dog felt fine the next day.

"Your child has great talents," I explain to my acquaintance, "which are not protected by correct orientation. You have to pray every day for your child to be kind and his love for God to be greater than his love for material things. It is necessary to go over your life carefully and change your attitude towards a lot of things. If your child's internal state is not changed now then his great skills can get blocked by the system of the self-regulating energy field and he will have a lot of problems in his life. Place the Bible on your tummy and let's see how the child reacts: if he doesn't feel good, if aggression appears then we have a difficult situation."

Luckily, the child reacted well to the Bible, - although, the New Testament was better received than the Old one.

My research shows that a child even before its birth actively interacts with the surrounding world and its spiritual and physical states are affected, first of all, by the mother's spirituality and ethics. A child is united with God on the fifth month of pregnancy and receives all its talents from Him. A woman is usually tested during the third-fourth months, which can come in any form, but the child's character and life depend on the result. The main thing is that orientation on spiritual values should always be greater than anything else.

My acquaintance, a doctor, approached me. I had healed her child from a rash by pointing at the source – a violation of the laws of the Universe a few years before her child was born. Just in case, she wanted to check that there were no other infringements. I found powerful deformations of her energy field structures, which had a negative impact on her fate. She was probably killing the love in another person with her words, because of that she and her children could face serious troubles. The woman couldn't remember anything like that and we spent about an hour searching for the cause. Finally we discovered it: she would often chat with her acquaintance – a young doctor, and once he came with his girl-friend whom he was in love with. After that this woman said to him:

"You know, you are not going to live together, she will leave you. She needs another man, not like you."

A little while after that, the young couple separated: the woman had unintentionally oriented his subconscious mind towards suppressing his feeling of love. Later it happened to him many times – the orientation continued to work in his energy field, destroying his relationships with women.

Quite often we don't think about how easy it is to harm somebody and – simultaneously – oneself. An innocent, from a worldly point of view, remark made by a woman harmed at least three people: her acquaintance, herself and her child, and this chain of events could have continued.

Recently, analyzing the cause for a woman's disease, I discovered structures of a curse from her mother in her energy field. It hadn't yet affected her health.

"Did you have a conflict with your mother in 1972?"

"Yes. She wasn't happy with me getting married."

"Was she against it?"

"Categorically. However I said that I would get married anyway."

I examined the karmic structures and saw an amazing picture.

"Please don't be surprised. Have you ever heard anything about previous lives?"

"Yes."

"In your previous life you died from cancer. Your present husband was your fiancé in the previous life and your mother was your mother. Following your mother's will you disowned him and didn't marry him despite the fact that you loved him deeply. In this life you faced the same test and you passed it. That's why everything in your life has been happy and even your mother's unintended curse has had no impact on you. However, your mother couldn't pass the second test. Strongly objecting your love and marriage, she repeated her mistake. If a cell fights the organism and tries to subordinate the organism to itself, it degenerates into a cancer cell."

She thought for a second and said:

"My mother died from sarcoma in 1975."

At that moment I thought about humanity – these days because of our pragmatism and groundedness we're rejecting Divine feelings more and more.

Major hereditary information is passed on not only through genes, but also through an energy field. A mother is inseparably linked to her child, therefore her emotions actively impact the child. If there was hatred and a separation with a loved one – this is a catastrophe for the child. Deformations of the structure of the woman's energy field determine many future miseries for the child.

Analyzing my patient's violations of the laws of preserving love I said:

"Your daughters accumulated so many negative programs that they may face infertility."

"Their horoscope says that they're supposed to be infertile." She answered.

"Astrology is secondary, the time of child birth is predetermined by the structure of his energy field, meaning by his karma."

During my work I had the chance to observe that a horoscope forecast can be altered under certain conditions.

A TV-reporter called me asking for a meeting. It turned out that she was an excellent conversationalist and an attentive listener. Her questions helped me organize material accumulated during the research process. It was very nice to talk to somebody, who was a professional in the bioenergetic sphere. I refused a public appearance, however, to avoid a stir and to quietly carry on my research.

We didn't have enough time to discuss all of her questions, so we agreed to meet the next day. That's when confusion started. We waited for each other for an hour in different places being completely sure that we agreed on that particular place. The situation was absurd, the reported called me and I tried to reach her in her hotel, at the end we managed to meet just an hour before she was supposed to leave. The woman was out of sorts and put a lot of effort into suppressing her resentment, she was successful and later we occasionally called each other.

In one of our conversations she mentioned that she was suppose to die in a few years, according to her horoscope. I analyzed her karmic structures.

"Based on the information I received, your child will die right after it is born. His head is the zone that will be injured. This will cause a stream of diseases and misfortunes, including mental disorders, and, unfortunately, your death two years after the loss of your child."

"So, the forecast of the horoscope is true, isn't it?" – she asked with an anxiety in her voice, which was difficult to hide.

"This is not about the horoscope, it's about your energy construction, in other words, your karma. The stars determine your destiny, because you were born at a certain moment predetermined by your energy construction. If you change your energy construction through spiritual development and aspiration for the Divine, then your karma and destiny will change as well.

I explained the major violations, which prevented her from rebuilding harmony in her energy field structure, and made the necessary corrections. She was pregnant at the time. A little after I got the feeling that a serious danger hung above her, so I called her.

"If you aren't able to eliminate the resentment that you have towards your husband, the mechanism of your karma will switch back on again. You stood the test during the third-fourth month of your pregnancy, you managed to block all resentments and complains against your husband, but now the situation is very dangerous for you and your child. You have to forget about day-to-day logic if you want to be healthy and happy."

For a while I watched her energy field from a distance: it remained harmonious and stable. The ecstatic mother called me after her child was born.

"You were right, my baby almost died. He was born with the umbilical cord entwined around his neck, as the doctors said."

An even more surprising confirmation came three months later, after the child went through an ultrasound screening. It was found that the child had microscopic haemorage in his brain. If the mother's complains and resentments weren't eliminated in time, the events could have developed in accordance to the scenario predicted by her horoscope.

The logic of love and forgiveness is above any astrology and fortune-telling. Aspiration for harmony, kindness and the Divine can override any negative karma.

The fate and character of a future child is formed in the information-energy field of his parents even before his conception. At the moment of conception the child's character and his destiny already exist and determine the child's future, thus if the parents have doubts about whether they need a child, this is considered to be an attack on these structures which can be deformed and even partially destroyed as a result. Rigid planning of a child's sex, or the unwillingness of either parent to have a daughter or a son, has an extremely negative impact on the energy field structures of the future child. Even the future parents' uncertainty whether they want to have a child, without even mentioning an attempt to get rid of it is the destruction of his fate, happiness, health and of his structures of communication and unity with other people.

A fifteen year old girl makes a statement: "I don't want to have kids". If she supports this program emotionally, then a few years later she may give birth to the seriously ill child. She will be the one to blame, completely unaware of this being the result of her careless statement.

Parents were expecting a boy, but a girl was born. They were upset for a day, but later they accepted the situation and now love their daughter enormously, however, she's often ill. The double program of destruction created by her mother and father hadn't disappeared and it had been working scrupulously in the child's energy field.

A husband offended his pregnant wife and she had a fleeting thought "It was a mistake to decide to have a child". Later he offended her again and again. The woman didn't wan't to continue her "happy" life. All of these feelings remained in the gentle, unprotected energy field of her son. Now he is poisoned by many medications, familiar with many hospitals, but his health is not improving.

It is very important during a child's sickness to create appropriate conditions for his correct recovery. What does this mean? Parents, first, have to think about the child's spirit, and only after that - about his body. Therefore, stuffing the child with medications and food can only harm him.

Recently I talked to the father of a girl that nearly died from a severe disease. I examined the energy field of the child before and after her sickness and was amazed. The powerful deformatio that caused the sickness was almost gone. I started to look for the reason for this successful recovery and found that it was the dad's love for his daughter. A significant part of the program of destruction and rejection of the Universe was neutralized by his love.

Yet we are talking particularly about love and not attachment. Love can heal, but attachment will only harm.

A lot of things throughout a child's sickness depend on the behavior, ethics and even the diet of his parents. The elimination of meat, alcohol, delicacies and overeating – all of this is even more important for the parents than for a child. All resentment and complains towards each other and towards the surrounding world around have to be let go. The state of the parents' spirit is the state of the spirit and body of their children.

To protect their child from diseases and misery, parents have to understand – the child's spirit must be healthy.

A young man sat in front of me sharing his problems. Two years ago he felt pain in his legs, so he visited massage therapists and made special baths. A few months later his feet were better, but his vision was getting worse quickly. This was a typical case. Rejection of a child before conception or during pregnancy – in words, thoughts or actions – deforms the energy field structures in three areas: the head, the first chakra and the legs. In this case it was the conjunction of significant violations from the paternal and maternal lines, thus the energy field deformation in the leg area, after traditional medical treatment, switched over to the next area – the head.

The processes, that used to take decades, now occur within just a few months. This is the reason for the confusion that medical doctors experince on an increasing basis in recent years. Before, when the disease localized in one place, it used to be medically treated for a long time and the person would recover (although, in reality, the disease would just move to another organ and gradually accumulate there), but now, due to the pollution in the karma of humanity, there is a different scenario. The disease is not strictly localized in one place any more, and during medical treatment it "floats" from one organ to another. Now not only part of the energy field of the person is ill, but the entire energy field becomes deformed. Focusing on the physical body that is focusing on the result and not the cause is meaningless and dangerous. Just as pointless is the incalculable spending of resources on fighting the disease, as opposed to the cause of it. This is not the medical doctor's fault, human thinking is imperfect and it childishly focuses on consequences, not willing to see causes. Those of us, who have been carried away by the benefits of civilization, remain as children who are more interested in bright colorful toys than in the necessary and vitally important things.

In the early years, religion used to give a person the correct stereotypes of behavior. A person knew one simple thing: "All is God's will". That was a wonderful block from negative subconscious influence on people and the surrounding world. Man could interfere with the course of events or resist them accordingly to personal interests, but inside he was obliged to maintain harmony with the surrounding world, because his soul is an energy field and particularly on the subtle energy field level it unites into a single whole with the entire Universe.

Sometimes confirmation that we are still far away from understanding the real causes of events in our lives comes in completely unexpected ways.

The chief medical doctor of one of the hospitals was familiar with the basic idea of the system of energy field self-regulation, but he wasn't in a hurry to apply them to his practice. However, one day, when he was sick and had a very high temperature for a few days that just wouldn't go down, he remembered about my research and began thinking: "God, I am very guilty in something. I don't know what I did wrong, I can't find the reason now, but please forgive me. Please allow me to understand and not repeat the same mistakes in the future..." Two hours later his fever dropped to 37.2 degrees.

Readers may get a very pessimistic impression and form the oppinion that, because of an accumulation of negative behavior, the position of humanity is terrible and hopeless. In fact, the situation of humanity is better than it may look at first, because of the existence of the mechanism of blocking and clearing karma.

First of all we need to comprehend that every person and every event that causes us to lose balance, is a part of the Universe, therefore, one's internal state should always be as close as possible to humility. The more subtle the energy field level, the less it depends on one's personality, the further it is from the logic of the body. Every person can help himself through correct behavior, correct understanding of the world and a correct diet. On top of that, there's a very important quality – inner aspiration.

In the early 70th in the area of Lake Ritz, I was taking a group on an excursion up to the Gegsky waterfalls. We walked slowly, without rushing. In about forty minutes we got to the top of the mountain and came to the edge of the cliff. From the huge height I could see the path we'd traversed, the narrow road from where we'd started our ascent. At that moment I got an association with human life, I realized quite clearly that man can achieve much more by constant, uninterrupted aspiration than by a one-time short-term dash.

A constant and uninterrupted striving for spiritual perfection is the most effective mechanism of blocking and clearing karma.

Today there is a lot of talk about the need to return to God. While saying "I believe in God" and attending church, a person can be very far from contact with the Divine. Believing in God is a process, where spiritual and physiological parts are combined.

If the cell starts to work in dissonance with the tasks of the organism, only for itself, then the process of pollution and disintegration will be triggered. Desire alone is not enough to restore unity with the organism. Hard, rhythmic and intense work is required to clean the cell and reestablish harmony.

Now the spirit and soul of humanity are unbelievably "polluted", seriously ill cells must die off and the processes we observe now reveals the beginning of this work.

Tireless conscious work to improve one's spirit and body is the only path to salvation. "We must strive, try and make all efforts every day and every hour to fight with ourselves ... to achieve something, but remember that tomorrow we can lose it, and once again will have to fight ... We shouldn't have any calmness or any pride .. . A person who obeys the commandments on the outside, but in his heart remains proud, judgemental and angry, is still far away from God," – said father A. Men in one of his sermons.

What is humility from the energy point of view? A person, who humbly accepts any life challenges, saves on an enormous amount of energy, that could be spent on fruitless complaints about the situation. All this energy in reserve can be used for inner, spiritual changes and for self-improvement.

Quite often I receive questions about whether it's possible to improve children's abilities and heighten their academic performance. A child's reluctance to study can be explained very easily. A mother during her pregnancy may refuse to feel love towards her husband, the child and the surrounding world. This action forms the program of rejection of the information field of the Universe, which blocks the child's ability to work with information. The child has trouble studying and he doesn't want to do it. Talented children are born to a loving mother, who doesn't allow herself or anybody else to doubt the feeling of love and unity with the Divine. Hence, children's abilities are the ethics of their parents and relatives. The less parents depend on their success, wellbeing and their own abilities, the easier it will be for their child to open up his abilities.

Not long ago I examined a child with a high level of subconscious aggression. That was his father's sister fault, the aunt's. Shortly before the child was born she committed an unethical act. That's why the term "family" always existed - it was based on the laws of bioenergetics. People of one family – mostly up to the fourth generation – have a particularly close unity on the energy field level.

Does the child's name have any influence on his destiny?

When parents choose a child's name it gets fixed in the karma of the child and affects his energy field structures. Some names are neutral, some names are benevolent, that have positive effects – this is possible to calculate energetically.

Sometimes it turns out that the name fixed in the child's karma doesn't correspond to the child's real name. The first time I saw it was when I was analyzing Yuri's problems with his mother's help. Somehow it always turned out that he should have a different name.

"Yes, at the beginning we wanted to name him Arthur, but later decided to call him Yuri" – his mother said.

I checked it from the energy perspective: the boy's karmic name was Arthur.

The name will bind the child with the fate of the person, after whom he was named. It is not accidental that before children were given the names of saints. The light, clean karma of the saint joined with the karma of the child, protecting him and working on his behalf. When we name children after any relative it is risky, because the mistakes and vices of this relative will have to be worked off by the child, which together with his name takes a part of his karma.

Once I heard a story that was a very convincing confirmation of our responsibility for each other. In one of the cities after my lecture a woman in her forties came to me and told me a story. She already had relatively grown-up children, when she decided to have another child. She'd probably accumulated many violations of the highest laws – a child was born, but died shortly thereafter. The woman didn't even bury the child, she left it in the hospital, and left without saying a word. Then in about a month one of her relatives died, later another one, then another one. It happened in a small town and friends started to look for somebody who could explain the reason and help the family. They went to see a famous witch-doctor, but she said that she could not do anything – the entire family had to be completely terminated. By leaving her deceased child in the hospital the woman had committed such a crime that the punishment was impossible to remove.

Love for children is related to be the highest feeling in the Universe, therefore, any violation against this love, such as the rejection of a child, reluctance to have a child or to be pregnant, not to mention abortion, especially a late term abortion of a child coinceived with a loved one (these violations can be in the form, not only of actions or words, but also thoughts) can lead to very serious consequences.

Two patients approached me. The woman had an ovarian cyst, and the man had severe back pain, prostatitis. Both of them had diseases associated with the imbalance of energy in the first chakra. The reason was the same: the woman advised her friend to have an abortion, and the man insisted on the termination of his wife's pregnancy. Meaning that verbal or mental desire to destroy a future person are violations of the laws, for which a person has to pay with his health and destiny.

A young beautiful lady had deformations of her energy field structures in the head and abdomen areas. This would indicate gynecological diseases in the future. They started to develop on the energy field level, when she had suicidal thoughts. After an abortion and suppression of her love to her lover these processes activated.

I am anxious about what is going to happen to us in a few years. We are absolutely illiterate. This girl will be treated with pills, but even if she gets into the best clinics in the world, nobody will cure her, because the root of her disease is an illness of her spirit, her soul. Anybody who has killed love in himself cannot be cured by medications.

A young woman had a serious skin problem. I told her the reason:

"Your grandmother during pregnancy had a desire to terminate the pregnancy and kill the baby."

"It's impossible," the woman responded. "My grandmother lost six of her children and only the seventh child survived – my mother."

I examined the cause for the childrens death. For some reason the grandmother didn't want her first pregnancy, she really didn't want it. The program of destruction of conceived life formed in her energy field. The strong feeling of hatred towards her future child, experienced only once, submerged into her subconcious and with every pregnancy, activated the program of destroying children. This program was present in the subconscious of the woman sitting in front of me, causing her serious skin problems.

Another patient asked me to help her son.

"My son has very sore legs, and sometimes it feels as if his legs give up on him, walking is very difficult for him."

I analyzed the cause.

"Five years after you were born your mother had an unwanted pregnancy, she tried to have an abortion and took some sort of poison. It didn't help and child was born, but her reluctance to give birth, her attempt to exterminate life and love formed deformations in your mother's energy field, which distorted and destroyed your energy field structures when you were five years old. And your son, who received them on the physical level, has to pay with his leg illness. The behavior of a woman five years before the birth of a child, during pregnancy and also during the period from his birth until puberty significantly influences the child's destiny and health. One of the ways of blocking negative programs, which are placed in our subconscious mind by our ancestors, is pennance during her pregnancy. The woman should ask for forgiveness for her ancestors and for herself, as a successor of their feelings."

A woman told me about her life. Actually, I led the narrative and she confirmed it.

"In 1957 you had an abortion, after which your heath began declining."

"Yes, after the abortion it was as if my destiny got distorted, I got tuberculosis."

"Five years after that you had a daughter?"

"Yes. After I gave birth to my daughter my health improved, the tuberculosis was gone. However, my child had a sever rash, and later – different skin problems."

Many women know that their health may improve after the birth of children. This is usually explained by the fact that the organism is activated during pregnancy, a renewal takes place. Certainly, the love that a mother feels for her child, ennobles her energy field structures and improves her physical condition. However there is one more reason, which people have no idea about. The mother passes her diseases on to her child, that is, the health disorders, through which a mother works off her karma, are passed into the energy field of her child and the child becomes sick. Karma is divided between mother and child. What indicates a first sign of trouble within the child's energy field structures? It could be a rash, allergies, frequent pneumonia in childhood, kidney diseases. Children's diseases are the deformations of the energy field structures that they received from their parents.

Some of my more difficult patients I "guide" constantly, control them from a distance. This is necessary to obtain a full picture of the disease and its cause. Influence and comprehension always come together. The soul is more difficult to heal than the body. Quite often it feels as if I am banging my head against a brick wall when I'm obliged to help a child with deformations in his character or destiny. In such cases I acutely sense the imperfection of my method and myself, as a healer and as a philosopher. However, after a lot of work, an enlightenment sometimes comes – and then I can take one more step in the development of the method.

Recently my acquaintance asked me to examine her friend's son. The boy was 2 and a half years old, but he had an incredibly harsh character. His desires had to be satisfied immediately, otherwise he would throw any available object at parents' and strangers' heads. In addition, the boy would get very upset if he missed.

Not long before the grandfather proposed to his grandchild: "If you are going to behave I will take you for a ride in the car". They went for a ride, came home, and the grandson took his toy-car and threw it at the grandfather's eye.

I invited the boy's father and mother together for a consultation, because the cause of the problem lay in both of them. They came with their boy. Within fifteen minutes he made a mess out of my studio, broke the light, got to the tape-recorder and broke the cassette. After that he found the oil paint tubes in my studio and started to throw them, with mixed success, at the heads of his parents.

There was a powerful justaposition of the negative family karma of his father and personal karma of his mother. During pregnancy the parents would often fight and felt antipathy towards each other, so the package of programs of destruction began to work autonomously and subordinated the child's conscious mind. Nothing would help to reduce his aggression. The most interesting thing was that parameters of his conscious and subconscious aggression were relatively low. Consequently, his behavior was determined by the worldview, behavior and the spiritual state of his parents at that very moment.

After two sessions I saw a stable improvement in the child's energy field structures, his spiritual structures had evened out. Still real change and renewal of the conscious mind takes about three months, so immediate results should not be expected. I warned parents that they would have to wait ten to fifteen days, because the balancing of the energy field takes time.

Five days later my acquaintance called:

"The boy is in the bad condition – he can't breathe, mother is panicking."

I talked to the mother and explain the reason for the occurrence with her child.

"You were expecting immediate results. The energy capacity of the soul is a thousand times greater than that of the body, consequently there's no visible changes so far. On the fourth day you allowed yourself to be upset with me and by doing so you violated the highest laws, and accordingly your child got worse. You have to understand that once I started work with your child I did everything I could to help him. Your complains hinder me, you and your child.

In a few days the mother came to see me and I explained to her:

"Every person in this life is born to develop and enhance his soul and spirit, through overcoming earthly temptations and miseries. Everybody has a main test in this life, which constantly repeats itself, a weak spot. In your previous lives you offended your husband, son and father. You simply "walked all over them". Therefore you were born in a family with similar karmic programs. This amplifies your programs and your task is to block them. The main challenges for you in this life should be resentment towards your husband and son. Your son has already been actively challenging you. This program might get even stronger in your husband. If you will be able to stand the test, not to hold resentment against your son and husband your karma will be removed, the challenges will be over and everything will be fine. If you won't, in addition to your present family miseries and illnesses, more misery will be added."

The woman's face took on a hopeless expression while I continued:

"The main temptation in your life is going to be desire to trample and offend your husband and son. If you will be able to resist – your son will recover, if not – get ready for punishment."

After that I checked their karmic structures one more time, did a session with the woman and her son and we took a break for a while.

In a few days my acquaintance called again:

"The mother and the child are both in a difficult condition, the child had suffocation and seizures again."

The reason is the same again. On Tuesday evening the mother had doubts whether I can help and heal soul, not just the body. She started complaining, denying the existence of the Divine and expecting quick visible results. This was immediately reflected in the child's behavior: he bit his friend in daycare. The mother was upset and had negative thoughts towards me – that was an attack on the energy field level. Because my energy field is balanced and it wasn't my fault this attack occurred, this attack returned back to her and struck the child.

Again I explained the reasons and restored the energy field structures.

"Would you like me to give you advice on how to be healthy and live long? Never have complaints against anybody or anything. Not against your Destiny, not against God, not against your past, not against people. On the outside you can do whatever, but on the inside, your complaint is a program of destruction of those you're complaining about. A cell can't have complaints towards its organism based on its own interests. It cannot because this represents a program of disintigration of the organism. This kind of cell will be torn away, and get sick. We are accustomed to complaining about everything and everyone: the government, a boss, co-workers, relatives.

A few days later I checked on the boy's condition. His mother said there is no noticeable improvement, but if a belt was shown to him he would stop throwing things. This tactic hadn't worked before. Thank God. The energy field was stabilizing, and the process was strengthening.

I watched the boy from a distance. I found one more reason for his aggression – suicide. The resentment of the parents, in other words, the program of mutual destruction initiated, within the child a program of self-destruction from the moment he was born. In order to survive, he turned this program, which was directed inwards, to the outside and returned it back to the authors.

After correction his energy field became softer, warmer. It looked like one of the most important causes for his behavior was removed.

Five days later I talked to my acquaintance.

"You know my friend was shocked, yesterday her son came to her and stroked her hand all evening."

In such moments, I understand my reasons for living.

When women ask me for help, I always check their children. A three minute talk can save a child from many years of challenges and illnesses. I inform the mother about the biggest challenge, from my point of view, her child can have and what his weak spots are.

I explained to a woman sitting in front of me, that the reason for her son's disease was her behavior during pregnancy. She was afraid that her husband might leave her and would kill her love for her husband. She even wanted to commit suicide. As a result, her child had a weak contact with the Divine, with the Universe. This affected his mental and physical condition.

I explained the reasons and warned her that during all trials the most important thing for her was to retain Divine feelings towards herself and her husband.

"You will always be provoked to reject the Divine, but you have to hold on."

"What about others, how do they live?" – she asked.

"Others have their inner reserves of love, which provide contact with the Divine. No matter how much they deny it on the outside, inside, in their subconscious they retain good contact. In contrast, you failed your test a few times already. That's why you have a strong tachycardia, pain in the pancreatic, colitis and gynecological disorders. Was my diagnosis correct?"

"Yes..." – said the woman, clearly amazed. "I was in the hospital half a year ago."

"Now there is a fibroma of the uterus forming in your energy field. If you are going to suppress your feelings because of fruitless complaints, it will manifest in reality."

"But how did people live before?"

"Do you know the expression: "Youth eats gingerbread and thinks that this is their daily bread". Before, because of the prophets and saints effort, who carried out the commandments and behaved correctly, we were firmly connected to the Universe, not putting much external effort into it. Today we have to earn it ourselves, by our own sweat and blood.

"Could you, please, tell me what the main test will be for my child, what kind of danger?"

I examined his karmic structures:

"His main challenge will be alcohol addiction."

The woman looked at me surprised:

"He is only three years old, but he practically shakes in anticipation when he sees a beer and insists on giving it to him. How can I help him?"

"First you should balance the child's diet. What is the meaning of his passion for alcohol? First of all it's that he is, to a certain extent, a slave of his desires, he can't resist them. This is because his spirit is grounded out.

If the spirit is elevated, the body and its needs can be controlled. The person owns things, things do not own the person. Do not allow your child to overeat. Overeating tramples the spirit into the earth."

The woman gasped:

"I can't refrain from cooking something tasty for him. When he was born and cried all the time, I constantly fed him so he wouldn't cry."

"His subconscious mind knew that he had a weak contact with the Universe and tried to improve this contact through crying. By giving him unnecessary food you have created a deceptive feeling of comfort. Getting used to it, he continued to look for the source of comfort in his body, not in his spirit. The needs of the Body started to outweigh the needs of the spirit, so the spirit started to deform."

"What should I do?"

"Do not overfeed, under no circumstances allow him to snack in between meals. Food should be served in minimum quantities, only at certain hours. Less Meat, as it "nails" one down to earth. Food should be monotonous, plant based. Exclude all delicacies, the child doesn't need them. He should be oriented, primarily towards the needs of his spirit. Reduce salt, as it increases subconscious aggression."

Never promise your child to buy a toy or delicacy. A child should dream about spiritual pleasures. Promise to take him to the theater or museum. A person dreams at the level of very subtle energy field structures. When we place material, earthly things into our dream, it really grounds us out. Make unexpected gifts. A mother who says: "If you are going to behave well, and study well – I will buy you this and that" makes her child a spiritual slave and the desired object is going to be his master. Unintentionally, she creates a program of destroying everything holy for the sake of material goods. That was the main reason for the downfall of previous civilizations.

The development of the spirit of the child is the best remedy against any negative tendencies.

Your behavior also greatly influences the child. If you suppress your Divine feelings towards your husband – it will immediately affect your child."

"You know, I think he's been bewitched. Recently he's been really angry with me."

"He's not been bewitched. The cause is in you. He reacts to your subconscious complaints with his conscious ones."

"I read in "Rabotnitca" ("Women-worker") magazine the tips of Russian sorcerers on how to bewitch somebody. They say that it is not dangerous."

"In order to bewitch somebody you have to demolish the Divine feelings in this person that guard him. Sorcery is an unnatural, violent process that damages the spiritual structures. The disintegration of spirit and destiny occurs also in the person bewitching. It has a catastrophic effect on the fate of children, especially on future ones."

The woman nodded her head:

"I always believed that you can't achieve anything by force."

"Of course. After all, what is magic? It is the use of the Divine potential for a selfish purpose, the subordination the highest karmic structures for short-term tactical interests.

When personal interest, personal survival becomes more important for the cell than the interests of the organism, when it starts to develop based on its own rules, different from the ones of the organism, then it can develop into an cancerous process.

Invasion into the subtle layers of the energy field, where everything is united, with the purpose of consuming, with material goals, triggers powerful programs of protection. Depending on the degree of penetration it initiates the mechanism of destruction of the individual, his family, a group of people or even, in the case of a severe violation, all of humanity."

"But if a woman wants to be with her loved one what can she do?"

"I am going to tell you "the biggest secret". Your spiritual development can not only "bewitch" your husband, but also make him really happy."

The woman said good-bye, but for a little while I continued to watch her aura and her child's aura. The energy field became golden, soft and warm. There was a feeling that all living things on Earth were joyful because of the enlightenment of their constituent.

A child had encephalitis. Three years before his birth there were difficult arguments in the family, the situation was close to divorce, also his mother and father frequently didn't want to live. These stable programs of self-destruction, which were cooperatively formed by both parents before the child's birth, were present in the child's energy field structure. Adults are more protected and the process of disintegration takes longer for them, but a child, who received two powerful programs of self-destruction from his parents, pays via encephalitis

The mother exclaimed in surprise:

"I can't believe that if this were removed my child would recover."

"Your child's health depends on the condition of his spiritual structures, and they are deformed. If they straighten out, your child will be in good health."

A woman suffered infertility. I diagnosed her and found that, judging by her energy condition, the cause was polycystic ovaries.

"You are the one to blame for your disease." The woman was surprised. "A few years ago you acted unethically and now this is the cause for your infertility. You killed love in a man who loved you, and you did it in a very harsh and abrupt way. Your connection with the Cosmos is blocked, also you have a low level of energy. Can you remember what happened?"

"I was engaged and we were getting ready for our wedding, but I met a man I liked a lot more and I married him instead. Do you think I was wrong? The person I got married to I loved much more."

I explain to the woman that a loving person experiences feelings, destroying which - in yourself or in another person - is a tremendous crime.

Following worldly logic, infertility can be eliminated by surgery. This is exactly what modern medicine is doing today. However, by destroying love and the feeling of the connection to the Divine, the woman destroyed the subtle spiritual structures in herself and in this man. If the child were to be born in these circumstances, it would have a mean character or a mean soul. The woman's organism blocks that by not being willing to give birth to the child that can get seriously sick, or die, or harm somebody else. If her spiritual parameters were low, she wouldn't even have infertility, she would just give a birth to the child with a "black" karma. But her spirituality and system of protection are sophisticated enough to get a sense of danger that threatens her children and grandchildren. We are accustomed to thinking that this is a disease and we fight against ourselves, against the organism that tries to protect the family from degeneration. I explained these rules to the woman and after that I could see that her energy field structures began to straighten.

"What should I do?" she asked.

"Above all, you need to realize that killing love is a crime, understand this not at the worldly level, but at the highest, spiritual level. When you understand everything your organism won't need to resist and set off the system of protection. The most reliable protection for your spirit against disintegration is the deformation of your body's crude structures. Their destruction forces a person to shift his frame of reference from his body to his spirit and that saves him. Disease prevents sin, as it's said in the Bible.

I remember a young woman with a similar illness – she had a complete obstruction of the fallopian tubes. The only reason for her problem – her grandmother had had an abortion. After that the tendency to kill children was only growing with every generation, and infertility was the physical protection of her organism from the appearance of imperfect, aggressive children.

After our conversation, the blockages started to disolve. I recommended that she be screened again. Doctors refused to do the tests again, arguing that this disease is not curable energetically and only the surgery can help her. The woman had to use a cooperative service (paid medical service) and in two weeks she brought the x-ray pictures. The blockages were completely disolved.

These cases just confirm that many gynecological disorders have their beginning on the energy field levels and often work as protection against the birth of defective descendants. By demolishing this protection, modern medicine, without any understanding the reasons for the disease, contribute to the appearance of a generation that lacks vitality, physically and morally. Rescuing a person from a particular disease, medicine opens up the floodgates for the development of negative processes, which reduce the overall immunity of humanity.

What is happening today to medicine reminds me the parable about the rider. A horseman was galloping along the road, when he saw a peasant.

"How can I get to N.?" the rider asked.

"You are going in the wrong direction." – the peasant answered.

"That's fine, I have an excellent horse!"

"But you need to go the other way," – the peasant tried to reason the rider.

"Don't worry, I have enough food for many days."

"The more food you have and the better your horse is, the further you are going to be from your target."

The more significant the achievements in medical science, the further we are going to be from our purpose.

We are used to thinking that the main defense system of the organism and body is the immune cell. We forget the simple truth: our spirit, soul and body are united. Consciousness and the subconscious are the energy field, the physical body – a different strain, the dialectical counterparty to this energy field. The highest priority in the system of an organism's defense is the defense of the spiritual energy field structures. Therefore, when the organism is facing the task of survival, the first priority is given to the survival of the strategic, spiritual structures that connect us to the origin.

We shouldn't forget the lessons of history. In ancient Sparta there was a custom: if a child was born frail and unhealthy or physically weak they threw him in the sea – in order to have healthy descendants. However, ultimately, this nation perished degenerating spiritually.

The philosophy of human perception of itself only as a physical body leads to the one-sided thinking of modern medicine. Their main methods of treatment - remove the ill organ, clean out, cut off, straighten up, correct. If man were only his body this approach would be acceptable, but man is simultaneously the energy field, moreover, the energy field is takes priority over the body. "I cannot fit between my hat and my boots", - said the poet Walt Whitman.

The laws of the human spirit are, simultaneously, laws for the body, but between them there is no direct correlation. As much as these laws can be similar, they can be just as opposite. When medicine starts to intrude into the area of the energy field, the human spirit, using the same methods it implements on the body – cutting off, removing, sewing together - this can lead to imperceptible (at the beginning), but very serious deformations of the spiritual structures.

The logic of those who cure the body; to do something first and then analyze it.

The logic of the spirit: to analyze first and then take action.

Trends in modern medicine – hypnotherapy, psychotherapy, extrasensorics – are attempts at a mechanical combination of the logic of the body and the logic of the spirit. In this case the latter dies. Because the philosophy and logic of spirit are the strategy, and ones of body are tactical, we can say that now the tactical, momentary success overshadows everything else. The expression: "After us there could be a flood and I wouldn't care" – this is the logic of the body. The question is whether there will be anything after us?

We learned how to relieve people from short sightedness using a surgical approach and we made a production line out of the method. Now not only many of our cities have branches where without any problems you can undergo surgery, but also other countries can benefit from this. However, did anybody analyze the results of this "victory"?

The cause of short sightedness is the distortion of the energy field in the head area, caused by a feeling of hatred, creating stable structures in the person's energy field. These structures don't disappear with eye surgery, they continue their destructive work in the energy field, and just move to other organs or parameters of the human spirit.

Surgeries to transplant or remove organs lead to similar outcomes. It is good if, at the same time, the person tries to heal his spirit, that is, to seek out and eliminate the cause, to understand his mistakes and to change something in his soul.

Even worse outcomes can be caused by illiterate energetic interference.

In A.Tarkovsky's film "Zerkalo" ("Mirror") there is a scene where a boy is healed from stuttering using hypnosis. I analyzed, what was happening within this method of treatment. A person that has a problem with stuttering has his destiny parameters deformed. I checked the boy's parameters before and after treatment by hypnosis - they were the same. Since hypnosis is unable to influence the cause of the disease and can only move it to a different location, I searched for the place to which it shifted. It turns out that the impact of the hypnosis shifted the disease into the future, the complete destruction of the child's karmic structures in three of his future lives. Isn't that a catastrophe?

Without accessing the root of a disease one can only transfer it – either to a different organ, or to his destiny, or to his psyche or his future lives, or just pile all the problems onto his children. The mechanics remain the mechanics. Disease cannot be cured without spiritual change.

I recall a parable a young doctor once told me. Allah summoned all the people and started to distribute punishments for their violations of the laws of the Universe. The doctor received the hardest punishment. He was outraged:

"Why? I am a doctor, I help people, I relieve them from suffering!"

Allah answered:

"I send disease to people for their transgressions, and you prevent them from understanding their sins."

I believe that religion, giving understanding of what correct behavior should be, in fact contributes much more to the humanity's physical health than medicine.

Recently I met somebody who was healed from a serious disease by a psychic: the person was walking on crutches, and after the treatment he could walk freely. The joy of the patient and his family was quite understandable.

While talking to this person I got the feeling that great trouble threatened his son. I tested the situation and found that the boy could die. The reason was that this man had a powerful program of destruction of sons from his paternal side, which had been blocked off by the leg disease.

After the treatment the program was revived, but now not only in the man's subconscious, but also in that of his son.

It is dangerous to eliminate visible problems without finding and simultaneously eliminating the root cause. Before, illness used to move from one organ to another, now extrasensory and new medicine (psycho-generators and equipment working on the energy field level) pushes the illness from the body – to the soul, fate, the mind and even to future generations and future lives.

A psycho-generator, while working with an information field, provides quick improvements on the physical and dense energy field levels and total destruction on the subtle levels. There was a woman on TV, who underwent treatment with a psycho-generator, which, as the ad promoted, "could replace a thousand psychics". I diagnosed this lady from a distance. I found a full recovery on the physical level and the transfer of deformations onto spiritual structures, fate and four future lives. Part of this deformation was left for the children.

If a disease is perceived as evil, then we will fight with it, moving it from one place to another. When disease is undertood to be an obstacle to spiritual degradation and the reasons for its appearance are eliminated, then the disease will go away by itself.

The imperfection of our philosophy and our understanding of the world leads us to self-destruction.

I was talking to my acquaintance about modern medicine in front of his son, a student of a medical university. The son had a severe headache and he took a few painkillers, but his headache wouldn't go away. I pushed one spot on his neck and shook him a little bit – his pain was gone. The young man had an interesting reaction:

"Father, why do I need to study in university when it is possible to cure like this?"

His father said that it is important to study anyway. I didn't say anything. An explanation would entail more than an two minute conversation...

Alternative medicine has not become a science so far. Alternative medicine doesn't know what it is working with. It is like a black box. The miracle of healing may happen, but there is a possibility that it may not. Quite often alternative medicine transforms into speculation. New healers, methods, schools come and go. Any discovery disappears utterly with time if they can't find its place in the system of worldviews.

The method, described in this book, permits the healing of many disorders years before the first signs of their appearance as physical illnesses. At one point of the development of this method I thought that karmic diagnostic could replace medicine completely. Later I realized the simple truth. The essence of this method is the prevention of events that may happen, but the conscious mind, focused on the body's needs, is unable to predict all of the processes. Therefore, we should not talk about rejecting modern medicine, but about a dialectical interaction between the medicine of spirit and that of the body (with a priority of healing and developing the spirit), about a radical change in the principals of modern medicine, about combination and interaction, rather than about the replacement of one worldview with another.

Taking care of only the physical body, medicine is moving further and further away from its main purpose – healing a man, because man is, above all, spirit and an energy field.

"A doctor-philosopher is like God" – Hippocrates said. Earlier philosophy, religion and medicine were a single whole. One person contained all the knowledge and practiced medicine. Now doctors are doing injections, performing surgeries, prescribing pills, executing instructions, etc. Is it possible to have another scenario? It is possible.

A doctor, who has high ethics and spirituality, treats not only the body, but simultaneously the spirit. Doctor Behterev said, if a patient feels better after visiting a doctor, that means that the patient has visited a real doctor. There are known facts when the mere appearance of a doctor in the room improved the condition of the patients. Unfortunately, during recent decades more and more attention in medicine is dedicated to the diagnostic equipment and treatments, rather than the doctor's character.

Recently my acquaintance approached me asking me to test new equipment, which was received by her research center. She was very excited when telling me about this equipment's potential, which by influencing the person's energy field allows treatment without medication. I decided to find out how this device works and, using his surname, diagnosed one of the patients that received treatment using this device.

He had served in Afghanistan and suffered from a stomach ulcer. His high conscious aggression and the feeling of hatred, which he was required to experience during the war, were the reasons for his ulcer. Powerful programs of killing people were formed in his energy field. His karmic structures were deformed. After treatment with this device the patient's energy field cleared, the deformation disappeared, and the physical condition of his organs improved significantly.

I began examining the more subtle energy of his organs and found that the energy of the endocrine center and first chakra became substantially worse than before treatment. I checked his parameters of spirituality, the degree of his love, aggression and the picture became clear: the ulcer healed, external aggression had dropped sharply, but subconscious aggression had risen substantially. It turned out that the ulcer was blocking the spreading of the program of destruction into the deeper layers of his subconscious. After the treatment, the aggression moved from the conscious mind into the subconscious. The parameters of spirituality and the soul decreased, and one of the most stable figures – the degree of love – which is responsible for our health in the future and our kids health, dropped to a critical level. Oveall, I saw a picture, which we observe all over the world: the destruction of strategic resources of the organism for the sake of temporary health for the physical body.

This device, as well as dozens of others, that have already been created or are just developing, is the best achievement of modern medicine and fully meets its requirements. Its philosophy is: it is necessary to remove the consequences without considering the causes. Devices straighten out the densest layers of karmic structures and push the disease inside, but don't eliminate it. The disease, after being pushed inside, will destroy not just a single part of the body or organ, but the immune system of the entire organism. Consequently, having overcome a single disease, modern medicine dooms humanity to gerneral, slow, painful degeneration and death. As disease functions to block incorrect behavior and thinking, much of it subconscious, removing these blockages speeds up the process of disintegration substantially.

Analyzing the energy field structures of society and humanity, as well as the information obtained from various sources, I came to the following conclusion: throughout the last 150 years the level of aggression experienced by humanity has increased, and, since the blockages between the conscious and subconscious mind are being destroyed, subconscious aggression is intensively growing. Our aggression is reaching the energy field level, the Universe. To stop this process, accordingly to the results of my research, the programs of self-destruction of humanity will be triggered in the fall of 1995. Only people with balanced spiritual structures will be able to withstand and survive in these conditions.

I really want this forecast to be wrong and to never be confirmed, but today there is very little hope for this.

The most promising and deeply influencing devices are the lepton psycho-generators. Perhaps, in the near future they are going to take the lead in the treatment of diseases. The research which I conducted showed that the energy field structures that contain genetic information are very well protected and energy influence does not reach them. There are only two exceptions: it is possible for a person with the highest abilities and for a psycho-generator.

Deeper penetration into the karmic structures in order to eliminate disease inevitably brings researchers into areas, where the program determining the genetic code of plants, animals and humans resides. This process might get out of control and then the mixing and "adhesion" of genetic karma will begin. At the beginning it will happen with similar programs, such as humans and animals, and then the complete mixing of the programs of all living creatures will occur. There is a possibility in the near future of the appearance of mutants, who will have the genetic structure of human beings and animals simultaneously. This type of mutation occasionally happens in nature, but after the information-energy influence their quantity is going to grow like an avalanche. The experiments conducted by Jiang-Kanchdzhen from Khabarovsk showed that, having even simple equipment, it is possible to connect genetic codes of different animals and plants. It is also possible that some researchers will attempt to experiment with the genetic code of humans and animals without any awareness that this is suicidal.

The danger of such experiments is that the program of "adhesion" of genetic codes of humans and animals, once realized, will exist and continue to develop in the information structures of the biogenosphere. As research shows, crimes committed against humanity are handed down as a program executable by many generations. The system of energy field self-regulation will step in to protect the information field. And if the destruction of the subtle spiritual energy field structures will not be blocked by diseases, then the most effective blocking mechanism will take effect – death.

A very illustrative case brought me to a new parameter of the system of self-regulation – love for oneself.

A woman that asked me for help had pretty good health. A minor disorder appeared in1978 when she experienced hatred towards another woman. The patient tried to recall it for a long time, but she couldn't remember anything like this. I had to explore deeper. It turns out that the hatred was directed towards herself.

"How could you hate yourself? Is it possible that you had thoughts of suicide?" I asked her.

"No..."

Although the woman said that she always felt a reluctance to live. Testing showed that reluctance to live and suicidal thoughts – are two different things. Unwillingness to live – is a lowered vitality. While experiencing this state petty troubles can cause suicidal thoughts to occur.

Previously I had thought that lowered vitality is a cause, but it turned out that it is a consequence and is determined by the family karma of the person, by the violations of the laws by his ancestors. In this case, the mother of this woman felt hatred towards another person, wished him evil, and this formed in her energy field an orientation for self-destruction, which is stored and transmitted to children, causing the slow destruction of the family line. The program works sluggishly, unnoticeably, creating a bleak inner outlook on life, sometimes obvious, sometimes not obvious, but gradually it cuts at the roots of the family line. A person with this type of orientation towards self-destruction is much more likely to commit an act that is dangerous for himself, is not going to appreciate his own life or the lives of others, and can harm a lot of people if they depend on him.

I examined the energy field of this woman's son –similar deformations were present there due to the suppression of love to himself, meaning that this mechanism continued to develop further. Despite the fact that the young man was in excellent health, he was in danger without even knowing it, because the orientation towards self-destruction, launched by his ancestors, continued its dirty work and could manifest in very unexpected and unexplainable, from a worldly point of view, ways.

A woman came to see me for the second time; during the first session I helped not only her, but also her husband. She was very happy with the results, but inside she didn't believe that it was possible to help her husband from a distance, without seeing him and talking to him. So she decided to give me a test. Taking out a picture from her purse, she asked me to find her husband. I showed her.

"That's correct. Can you also find a person who died five years after this picture was taken?"

I could see right away a person whose destiny parameters were distorted, so I pointed at him on the picture. She was surprised:

"How did you know?"

I just waived my hand tiredly in response. I am a professional. There is no miracle here, this is hard, intense work, the result of long-term work developing and improving my abilities.

A few months ago my acquaintance approached me.

"I am panicking," she shared. "I have a friend and we've known each other for quite a while. Suddenly, today she came saying that she loves me, that she is experiencing unusual feelings towards me. Do you think she might have some sort of disorder?"

I examined the situation and said that, unfortunately, there was a disorder present.

"Is it possible to remove it somehow? I don't know what I should do now, because she's just going mad."

This was a very interesting case, and I began to explore this topic. Is it possible that the deviations in sexual orientation be conditioned by karma? The whole world treats homosexuality as a norm now, not only do clubs exist, but also the belief that this is absolutely normal. If this is the result of a deformation of the karmic structures and there is a possibility to correct them that means that we can talk about a specific disease.

I checked the karmic structures of the woman and found that the reason for this deviation lay in something that happened to her grandmother: once her grandmother's best girl-friend, to whom she was very attached, offended her. The friend, with her words and some kind of action, destroyed their friendship and caused strong emotional stress for the grandmother. This subconscious mind set of destruction of love towards women was passed down by inheritance, and in order to compensate for it, the subconscious mind increased the degree of attachment to women. That was how this event manifested in the form of deviation. I corrected these structures from a distance and could see how the woman's feeling changed.

"Now everything will be fine. There shouldn't be any more excess, your friend will behave completely differently now."

And so that happened. Her friend visited a day later and said, completely confused, that she couldn't understand how this could happen.

We can't even imagine how distorted our present view of the world is. Homosexuality can appear as an attempt to compensate for the dying love of one person to another. A human has to love all people, and sexual love is only a small fraction of universal love, love towards people as Divine creatures, beautiful parts of the Universe. If this inner humanistic love to people is absent, then homosexuality can appear as a way to compensate for it. However, this is a disease, this is a deviation from norm, this is a result of the fact that love is dying in us.

The fading of human love leads to an increase in the number of homosexuals – and this further demolishes love, disintegrates spiritual and physical structures. A woman, violating her biological orientation, provokes the degeneration of her descendants at energy field level structures. A man, realizing his homosexual inclination, receives the disintegration of his spirit, soul, fate and decreasing energy levels. The disintegration of karmic structures in men is less apparent than in women.

However, in general, homosexuality demolishes the energy field structures in people, which are responsible for the immune system, for resistance to cancer, for the health of descendants. Active homosexuals suppress the love and life in their partners, their children may be prone to violence against other people and to cruelty. Passive homosexuals demolish the love and life in themselves, and their children may become the victims of various crimes, or may have the program of self-destruction in their energy field structures.

Just for comparison's sake I will list the parameters of loving people: spirituality, soul, destiny, degree of love should have the highest values; subconscious aggression – as low as possible. By loving each other man and woman improve their karmas, heal themselves and their future descendants.

The Third Reason

Any phrase contains a cluster of information. A word isn't powerless, it's a program, an organism that interacts with other programs in an energy field.

When I read ancient Indian philosophy, I was amazed by the assertion that the spirit is stable, and the body by comparison is just an illusion, I couldn't believe it. Lao-Tzu's notion that everything weak and defenseless wins over the hard and strong seemed to be a metaphor to me. But using spiritual methods of healing in my work, it is impossible not to be amazed by the degree of dependency of our body on the spirit, on the biofield structures.

Quite often in everyday life we allow ourselves to speak badly of other people, of ourselves, of our own fate. It turns out that this habit destroys teeth. I examined dozens of cases and found that the most dangerous is unkind remarks about close family, relatives, wishing harm to people close to us, in these cases the karmic programs of our parents and from our past lives contribute to the destructive impulse. The most dangerous is dissatisfaction with oneself.

The causes of periodontal diseases are unkind words towards the father, burdened karma and an incorrect diet. The regular use of greens in one's daily meals helps to find emotional balance and reduce subconscious aggression. Similar to that, the effectiveness of phytotherapy is determined primarily by the fact that it influences the spiritual structures and not just the physical.

What is so dangerous about negative-thinking and negative-language?

When we think about somebody an energy bridge appears between us and the person about whom we think, there is an exchange of information and energy – therefore, any negative thought is an energy attack and can cause harm. Even an inner agreement with a negative person can be dangerous. Slandering, negative thoughts about people causes trauma and, respectively, destroys ones own karmic structures. Words empower any program.

Currently, the energy of the Earth is such that even an unkind thought about somebody is enough to cause them harm. By analyzing a large number of cases, I came to the conclusion that a few centuries ago humanity started actively drifting away from the principals of world harmony, so now the information field of the Earth is overloaded with negative programs. When a man thinks about somebody unkindly, communal negative karmic layers attach to it. In this way it is possible to harm somebody, without even any intention of doing so. We attack and destroy each other subconsciously, often without even realizing it. An avalanche-like process of self-destruction takes place, which doesn't even require any negative emotions - there is already enough negative potential accumulated by humanity.

Today it is not enough to be good and not harm anybody. The Subconscious mind is already so deformed, that even a lack of harm inflicted is not a sufficient condition to save the soul and body. Given the present situation the main condition for survival is conscious, purposeful work to change oneself. It is not adequate just to be good, one must be actively good. Any kind and honest person is likely to perish, not to mention those who violate the highest laws. The ideals and commandments that people followed for thousands of years are forgotten today, pushed to the background, therefore, people have to consciously and actively work to rebuild their spirituality, humanity and understanding world harmony. *"Love your enemies"*, this is a call to the spiritual nature of humans not to respond to an attack with an energy attack. The objective for an ethically educated person is to never allow negative feelings to get into the subconscious. A person that starts his day with the prayer: "God, grant my relatives and acquaintances health, and patience for me", blocks himself from a lot of violations.

This is an example of the function of just one phrase. A young man offended a young girl and she said: "I will never forgive this". I examined what happens: a program of destruction or separation is formed – that which is called an "evil eye" in bioenergetics. Today any categorical or flat statements unfortunately, inflict harm on oneself and the other person.

A man came to consult with me complaining about weakness and lethargy. His energy variables were very low. Testing them allowed me to find the reason:

"You have a neighbor and you get into fights with her quite often?"

"Yes."

"You resent her and this feeling distorts your energy field and consequently your energy drops. But the worst part is – you talk negatively about her."

His lethargy disappeared soon after we removed the violation and his energy field balanced out.

Negative judgment about somebody causes a significant drop in energy. When a man slanders somebody else he harms the person, and also harms himself, because it causes a deformation, demolishing of his own energy field structures, resulting in a loss of energy. Nasty thoughts about somebody, negative words about him – this is an attack on the energy field level and the price for this is known: *"Don't judge and ye won't be judged, for with what judgment ye judge, ye shall be judged, and with what measure ye mete, it shall be measured to you again"*.

The trauma caused by negative language initially might not even appear on the physical level, it's not necessary that a disease will develop right away. The disintegration of the subtle structures might begin, however, the person feels perfect, but the deformation of his energy field structures occurs, which have tremendous capacity though it might not show up right away. But later, when troubles begin, his relatives or children might become sick, for example, it's very unlikely that he will figure out that the reason for these problems was his negative language.

We are killing ourselves without even noticing it. **Negative language shortens our lives, destroys us physically and spiritually.**

I wanted to find out what is the main thing that all long-livers have in common? Their diets are varied, as well as their life style and behavior; the only thing that they all have in common is their good nature. It turned out that good nature is the absence of an energy attack on people and, their corresponding invulnerability. We die early because we constantly destroy the soul and body. The Japanese are a nation that lives to old age and, at the same time, the most polite people on the planet.

The most dangerous is negative language against loved ones. The degree of unity on the energy field level can vary, but it is the highest between people that love each other. The feeling of love spiritually elevates a person, therefore, any negative influence on this feeling is extremely dangerous.

While working on this book we often got together at the publishing house, and there was a young author from Moscow, Slava, at one of these meetings. There was a discussion and testing of the new literature he brought with him. Slava told us that during one of his trips he met a very interesting clairvoyant, possessing a unique ability. He could say to his patient: "Go home, there is a spell-bound pair of scissors buried under your front gate on the left side. After you dig them out, everything will be fine"; and, sure enough, the person would go home and find scissors under his gate. During the conversation devoted to Slava's book it turned out that this clairvoyant couldn't help Slava. "You have a very strong Guardian Angel, I am not allowed to heal you" – he admitted to Slava.

We sat there, talked and, suddenly I felt that somebody was taking my energy. By testing I figured out that it was Slava's work. Right away I corrected his energy field structures, but noticed that some women in the room started feeling unwell. I checked Slava's parameters and found that he carries the program of destroying women in his subconscious.

That was completely unexpected for him.

"Could you please tell us about your personal life?" – I inquired.

"Not very satisfying. Eight years ago my wife and I broke up and so far I have no plans to get married again."

I explained to him that the reason for his unsuccessful marriage was his program of destroying women, living in his subconscious and formed by his dad before Slava was born. After the correction his energy field became harmonious.

I held a diagnosis and healing session at a factory.

One of the workers came back after two hours complaining that she had a severe pain in the area of the third eye. I checked the reason for the pain – there was a subconscious negative wish and the program of destruction.

"You said something negative about me right after our session," – I explained to this woman.

"How could I, I didn't say and didn't think anything negative about you. I just said: "Poor Sergey Nicholayevich, he is so tied, his face is almost green".

"You caused me harm with your pity".

"Do you mean that we can't feel sorry for somebody?"

"We can help somebody, empathize, but we can't feel sorry for them. Pity is directed towards the body and can harm a person's spirit and soul. Once at my session one patient felt sorry for another one and two months later she got the same disease, she had to have surgery. You forget that these days everybody has a high level of energy, therefore any mistake can turn into a serious deformation of the energy field structures with all subsequent consequences."

Disease is not bad thing, but a way to stop the programs of spiritual disintegration. When you feel sorry for somebody, you disagree with his disease, his misfortune, you think only about the consequences forgetting about the reason, and by doing so you support the disintegration of his spirit. It is a very fine line, when external sympathy, willingness to help gets inside, it can turn into its opposite. Inwardly we have to acknowledge the legitimacy and rationality of the existence of the disease as leverage in spiritual development, and accept it humbly. This duality in attitude – inner humbleness and external care and compassion – enables living in harmony with the Universe, without complaint. Disease has never been only good or only bad, disease is always both at the same time.

The Fourth Reason

Studying the problem of vampirism I tried to figure out why somebody becomes a "vampire". Vampirism is absolutely not a harmless exercise. The interaction of people on the subtle, energy field level is much more complicated then we can imagine. Vampirism is not only the taking some amount of energy, a breach of the energy field shell and creating conditions for the consequent energy leak, it also damages the subtle energy field structures, which can lead to the deformation of the karmic lines of destiny, health and psyche. I have repeatedly observed examples of mental disorders that appeared after losing a large portion of energy.

Somebody who begins to use someone else's energy will have his connection with the Cosmos cut off, and this in turn leads to a general decrease in energy. This process is a very difficult to stop, it condemns the children of the "vampire" to be seriously ill, due to the fact that they are born with their channels of connection to Cosmos already blocked, they may either become victims of vampirism and their body will be subject of destruction, or become vampires themselves and continue further destruction of their souls. All of that said, vampirism – is a very complicated and rather serious topic. Here are some examples from my practice.

A woman had an appointment with me. It was her third visit. Diagnosis of her daughter from a distance showed that one of her music school teachers was taking her energy. The reason has a karmic nature: there was vampirism on the paternal line, the girl's shield was penetrated and therefore, her energy was being taken. I tested her father and found that, indeed, he was taking energy, although it wasn't his fault, but rather his dad's. His father behaved very selfishly towards his mother, suppressing, keeping her down, so that she would throw her energy to him.

Selfishness and cruelty lead to disconnection from the Cosmos and then the person has no choice but to take energy from other people. This, in turn, demolishes the protection of his children, they start getting seriously ill and they might have mental disorders or other problems. In this example, the grandfather's ego significantly worsened the sons and granddaughter's karmas.

A young man told me his story:

"One trouble making drug-addict, a completely degraded person and professional thief, used to constantly come to my house and try to break the door, smash light bulbs, tear off telephone wires - in other words, demonstrated his aggression. Last time he came and started pounding on the door. Standing behind the door, I began praying for him. At the beginning the trouble-maker, as usual, tried to break the door with shouting and a lot of noise, but suddenly he got quiet and I heard him quietly leaving. It had never happened before. Usually, when leaving he would bang on the neighbor's doors, break glass and light bulbs. What happened to him?"

Testing showed the powerful wholesome effect of the prayer on the spirituality, mind, fate and behavior of the trouble-maker.

It turns out that a person, praying for the soul of another person, has a much stronger influence than a professional psychic, because prayer has an effect on the subtle structures.

I examined the results of the energy parameters of the hooligan before the prayer: a high level of aggression, mental disorder and a very low level of connection with the Cosmos. What determined the trouble-maker's behavior? Subconsciously he felt a high energy level in this young man, he would set up a scandal, irritate him to receive someone else's energy.

After the prayer he also received energy, but that was energy of a different quality, this energy started to transform him. Perhaps, it was unexpected and incomprehensible to him, so he got quiet and left.

Something very unusual happened to him, he could not figure out his own state.

The results of testing after the prayer: his spirituality didn't change much, despite the fact that the influence was spiritual, - that means that some other parameters were influenced – in general, it was his behavior and mental state. This person became almost healthy mentally, although his body parameters, meaning his physical state, slightly worsened. Sometimes prayer can have a negative impact on the body parameters, if the body and spiritual structures are in conflict. When the spirit rises the body may get weak temporarily. However, the behavior and character of this person became consistent with the norm.

The main reason for the mental disorder, the low level of connection to the Cosmos and aggressive behavior of this person was his father's behavior, his repeated attempts to commit suicide. The program of self-destruction, which had been initiated by his dad, determined the sad destiny of his son. After a correction of the karmic structures of the father, his son's connection to the Cosmos rose sharply. The young man's prayer changed the trouble-maker's behavior, but his connection to the Cosmos was only improved after I made a deeper correction.

It was interesting to continue the study further.

"At what time did he usually come?"

"It may seem strange, but he always used to come during the happiest moments of my life, at the most inconvenient moments. That was always awful and painful."

"Is this accidental? No, it's not. He would appear during the happiest moments because spiritual uplift fills the human body with energy. Perhaps he felt it instinctively and wanted to receive this energy."

How do people that need energy usually act? They irritate and torture their victim, seeking different ways to subdue, because it is difficult to take something from an equal, while it is much easier to take from the weak. Why, for example, would somebody be a sadist? His parents would deny their unity with the world, their highest feelings. This would cause the complete blockage of the channels connecting this person with the Cosmos, causing disintegration and degradation of the energy field structures - as a result, there is no way for him to get energy, apart from taking it away from somebody else. If this were a child, he would start irritating his mother, annoying her. She would constantly become angry and yell at him thus giving him energy. The child would hurt and bully his classmates, beat animals, receiving energy in this way as well. He would laugh and bully adults – again achieving the same purpose. When one person leads another to physical or spiritual suffering – this is a form of vampirism.

Sometimes, however, the mother creates the conditions for the development of vampirism in her child. For example, after completing an accelerated course of contactless massage, at any occasion when her child gets slightly ill she would start using the energy of her hands to provide crude, physical, but not spiritual energy. In other cases she would constantly get irritated with her child and yell at him, also giving him crude energy and by doing so teaches him to be an energy consumer.

A mother, who prays for her child's health, also gives her energy to a child, but this is spiritual energy that heals him and helps him to develop correctly. Health does not happen without love.

Intentional vampirism, meaning the direct taking of energy, is also possible, but a certain knowledge of bioenergetics required to do it, the ability to feel energy.

For the person with disintegrating spiritual structures it is more and more difficult to connect with the Cosmos to replenish his energy, therefore such a person consumes others energy more and more frequently. This is how the avalanche-like process of vampirism and disconnection from the Cosmos starts. Often enough, it ends with a severe disease. A "Vampire" becomes like a drug addict, who pays heavily tomorrow for pleasure received today.

Sometimes ill-prepared psychics can take energy from their children and relatives without awareness of having done so. The latter become sick because of this.

Few people know the seriousness of the punishment for vampirism and how difficult it is to get out of this state. A victims energy field structures are deformed when he is under the bioenergetic impact of an energy seizure. This deformation may persist for a long time and result in disease for the victim. The aggressor, his children and relatives are going to be accountable for this. One of the best ways to protect oneself from an unethical person, who is attempting to take one's energy, is prayer, because it also helps the aggressor, rebuilding his deformed spiritual structures. *"Bless them that curse you... and pray for them who spitefully use you, and persecute you..."*

Here is another example of vampirism. A woman asked me to help her youngest daughter and granddaughter, her oldest son's daughter. I examined the woman's daughter first. She was fourteen yours old and studied at school. She had a strong deformation of her energy field structures in the head area, which were caused by a man's vampirism.

"Does the girl have frequent headaches?"

"Yes."

"Is she pale, does she tire easily?"

"Yes, she gets very tired, especially in her math class."

"You know, it has nothing to do with math. Some man is taking her energy, quite possibly a teacher. And the reason for this is that her father used to take the energy from you a while ago. So the girl's protection has been breached and she can fall prey to any "vampire".

After that I checked the granddaughter's energy field. The granddaughter was also a vampire victim. And the cause was with her dad, he was taking energy from his wife. But that was not the end of the chain. The dad had to take the energy, because his mother, the girl's grandmother, who was sitting in front of me, took energy energy from some man in 1962. Five years later, her husband began taking her energy, her protection had been breached. The process where "the victim provokes the offender" had begun. The grandmother breached her own protection, and after that the chain reaction took place – her son, daughter and granddaughter were suffering. They were destined to take or submit energy leading to disintegration of the subtle energy field structures and gradual physical destruction. All it took was only one unethical act by the grandmother and the result was physical and spiritual disintegration for the whole family. Irresponsibility on the energy field level ends in tragedy.

The next patient was a young woman with numerous problems. I explained to her how she violated the highest laws and how it affected her character, destiny and health. Her channels of connection with the Cosmos were blocked, and this was her father's fault, because he refused unity with the Universe and as a result his daughter had a reduced level of energy. The young girl confirmed that her dad was an atheist and materialist.

"It has nothing to do with him believing in God or not", - I explain. - "A human being is a cell of a unified organism, and he has to live accordingly to the laws of this organism. If he doesn't understand this, his children are doomed to degeneration – first spiritual and then physical.

I checked the energy field structures of the girl. Because her energy level was low and connection with the Cosmos was minimal, she was taking my energy. The young woman didn't feel it, but she noticed that children didn't like when she would pick them up. The energy field of a child is unprotected and it is very easy to take their energy, but his intuition still protects him. Let's recall, in earlier years small kids were always hidden from stranger's eyes, so that unethical people could not harm them.

Once during my lecture the topic of vampirism came up. I explained the mechanism – how self-destruction occurs when a person starts to take energy from other people. That was a lecture for psychics. One of the listeners, quite a self-confident young man, stated that he has an excellent remedy against "vampires". I was curious and asked him to share.

"When a 'vampire' attempts to take away my energy, I imagine myself as an abscess, let him take it."

"If 'vampires' attack you constantly, with this kind of 'protection' you will become this 'abscess'. We become that which we imagine. I wouldn't recommend to use this advice. If you feel that somebody is taking your energy, you can ask that this person be given Divine love and energy, which will transform him, cleanse his soul and connect him with the Cosmos."

Later I checked this young man conditions: his parameters such as spirituality, soul, behavior, all had negative values. This represents a complete degradation of the subtle spiritual structures.

If one asks that a "vampire" be given Divine love and energy, then the values of his parameters of spirituality increase significantly. Conscious help saves one who intentionally or unintentionally has taken energy from other people.

This example is representative of the fact that violence, which is often automatically transferred from the physical world into the spiritual, into the world of bioenergetics, is suicidal. The person can almost never see his degeneration. Having committed several cases of violence on the spiritual level, a person doesn't feel how his soul disintegrates, because he is used to watching, primarily, what happens with his body.

And the most important. In the "vampire"-victim tandem the victim always wins, because vampirism is the signal of the low level of connection with the Divine. Vampirism pushes the victim towards higher energy, the energy of spirituality. The "vampire", in turn, experiences the opposing process – the progressing degradation of his subtle spiritual structures that receive Divine energy.

The Fifth Reason

This is a well known saying: "Do not speak ill of the dead". Why not? Connections between the subtle world of the dead and our, physical world are possible, and if they occur it can be dangerous for both worlds.

"Adhesion" of energy fields between the living and the dead can occur when the highest laws are violated. Religion and funeral ceremonies in all nations in the world are focused on separation of the energy fields of the living and the deceased, for example: the burial service for Christians, incineration of the body for Indians etc.. These all assist in the energy field separation and the successful transition of the energy field structures of the deceased into the corresponding hierarchy of the Universe.

If a person resents the deceased it has a negative effect on him and can lead to various diseases, mental disorders, changes in character.

If a dying person holds onto resentment before death this can also lead to an "adhesion" of energy fields – this is probably why the tradition to fulfill a person's last wish is well respected.

If a woman had an abortion before giving a birth to a child, then the energy field of the deceased fetus can join with the energy field of the later born child, and child can be very unhealthy, experience fears or obsessive behavior.

Once we met a family while on vacation by the sea. They had two kids. The youngest girl was afraid of heights and would constantly scream at night. I diagnosed the problem and found that the mother, before having this child, had had an abortion and the energy field of the unborn child had joined with the energy field of the girl. I explained this to this woman, she understood and went to church, where she asked for forgiveness for the unborn child. After that, the energy field of her daughter was restored and she stopped screaming at night.

That was one of the first times when I felt the great power of the word, how effective it can be in healing.

A woman came to consult with me. Her energy field had a severe disturbance, a so-called "evil eye". She had actually bewitched herself - her negative attitude towards her grandfather, deceased long ago, was the cause. Since the human energy field contains information about all relatives, her negative feelings towards the deceased grandfather were present in the woman's energy field and deformed it. The resentment towards her grandfather was actually directed at herself. It is very dangerous to feel resentment or hate people, with whom one has a close energy relationship – that is ones parents, children, loved ones, relatives. The stronger one's love and attachment, the more dangerous the negative feeling towards beloved people.

In Moscow I was asked to diagnose a woman who was feeling quite ill. She thought that she might have the beginnings of diabetes, but doctors denied it. But they also wouldn't give an explanation for her feeling ill. I looked at her energy field and found that energy was pouring out of her body in the area of her solar plexus. I began searching for the reason.

The woman said that about a month before her grandmother, who had been a professional witch-doctor, had passed away. Before her death she had wanted to see her granddaughter very much, but the woman didn't make it in time. The grandmother died without seeing her granddaughter. The woman had a very strong connection with her astral body, that is why there was such a substantial loss of energy. One of the signs of this type of puncture is constant uncontrollable fear.

I tried to figure out how this could be eliminated. I suggested lighting a candle in church for the peace of the grandmother's soul, but woman had done it already a number of times. Then I decided to do an experiment. I can communicate non-verbally with the souls of the deceased, feel their attitude towards living people. I thought that the grandmother might have wanted to pass something on to her granddaughter before her death, so I decided to arrange their meeting. I concentrated, called the soul of the deceased grandmother, established the energetic connection between them and left the room.

When I was back a few minutes later, the woman told me that her hands had turned palms up and something happened. The woman's energy field was fully restored and the feeling of fear disappeared completely. That means that the grandmother used her chance to accomplish what she wanted to do.

After a while the woman noticed that her health improved, as well as the attitude of people towards her. I assume that some transmission of knowledge and experience was completed. However, I have never repeated this kind of experiment.

My next patient asked me to help her daughter. She was seeing strange dreams. Her grandmother, deceased a year and a half before, would always be in them. The grandmother would talk to her granddaughter, give her advice, and discuss events that happed after her death. Until forty days after her death, she kept asking her granddaughter in the dreams:

"Tell me how I was buried, because I don't remember anything."

When the grandmother's things were transferred to the vacation home, she reproached the granddaughter for doing so:

"Why did you take my stuff to the dacha?"

The granddaughter tried to explain that since the grandmother died it was not necessary to keep her things at home.

"No, I am not dead yet." – the grandmother said.

This is a typical example of an energy field adhesion between the deceased grandmother and the granddaughter, and the reason for this was the granddaughter's strong resentment towards her grandmother. Resentment towards a deceased person is one of the reasons for disturbance in the normal blocking of the energy fields.

Sometimes a person who died a long time ago, has information about events from the material world and even can influence their course.

Once an interesting story happened to me. I met a woman that possessed incredible abilities in bioenergetics. Many years before, her dad had passed away and suddenly he had started appearing regularly in her dreams. She was scared at the beginning, but later she got used to it and they started communicating. He would often warn her about potential troubles and give her advice.

I was getting ready for my vacation in the South, but I wasn't in good shape. I felt that something might go wrong. I spoke with this woman and asked her to ask her father to help me, protect me if something unexpected were to happen.

At the beginning everything was fine, but one day, I went for a swim and got far out to sea. Suddenly I felt such a sharp pain in my knee that I couldn't imagine how I was going to get back. It was a joint capsule sprain in my right knee.

It happened because before the trip I took a great offence at a woman. Using ordinary logic, her actions were dishonorable. It was a test I didn't stand, and consequently, misfortune, trauma, or disease had to happen. I couldn't handle this deep resentment properly, it grew, turning into hatred and my family suffered the most from it. I had a feeling that something strange had gotten inside of me, subdued me and inflamed a dull hatred. By rights, I should have faced serious misfortune in response to my violation of the highest laws. After testing the situation I found that, thanks to indirect assistance from my acquaintance's father, I avoided serious misfortune, and got away with just an injury.

When I returned my acquaintance told me that she saw her dad in her dream – he was sitting next to me, smiling. I was smiling too and my right leg was awkwardly off to the side.

Later, analyzing karmic fields, I realized that her father had managed to transfer the punishment, which was supposed to be in the form of misfortune for my relatives, to my knee injury, as if he had deflected the misfortune, causing minimal damage. I couldn't figure out how he was able to help at the time.

The Six Reason

Not long ago, while working with a patient, I discovered a significant factor that affects the health and destiny of many generations of descendants. Perhaps my karmic energy field wasn't clean enough to receive this information. The essence of this is as follows: any thoughts about suicide are very dangerous and destructive for a person and his descendants.

I was healing a woman who suffered terrible headaches and no medications would help. Doctors weren't sure about her diagnosis, so she turned to bio-energetics. When I looked at her karmic lines, it turned out that her father had done something bordering on suicide. The program of self-destruction continued working in the woman's energy field, creating the strongest deformations of her energy field. The desire for self-destruction, programs of unwillingness to live, can remain in a person's subconscious for many years. The program this woman received from her father was so powerful that her organism had to use severe headaches to block it. After two sessions correcting her energy field structures her headaches began diminishing.

I was interested to find out how common this program was and found that, to my regret, every second patient has the program of subconscious suicide in his energy field. It can manifest in the form of apathy, depression, sometimes as a burst of aggression the person can't control. The condition, which doctors call depression, is a hidden unwillingness to live and it can provoke different diseases, it can deform one's fate, one's character, and can make a person's life very difficult.

What could be the reason for a person's sluggish reluctance to live? First of all, that would be the program of self-destruction, formed in the energy field when one of the ancestors was reluctant to live for a long time or attempted to commit suicide. Even if it happened three or four generations ago, the program is very stable and transferable to descendants.

Also this program may be a consequence of the reluctance of parents to have children.

The human energy field is protected from the surrounding world, but absolutely open to parents. The slightest violation on the parents part during pregnancy in relation to a future child forms the program of destruction in his energy field. This program is long-lived because it is initiated by the parents.

Dissatisfaction with the fact that a child is small and weak, or is often getting sick, displeasure with his sex, appearance, the caprices of the born child - if all these are not surpassed by the parents love, comprehension that child is a gift from God, they get inside, into the subconscious mind, and then the flywheel of destruction is launched. As a result, long-lasting fixations on negative emotions towards the child go into the subconscious mind and start developing independently, meaning that the conscious mind loses control over these emotions and doesn't understand their danger.

The energy field of the parents starts to destroy the energy field of the child. Immediately two programs are launched in response within the child - the program of destroying parents and self-destruction. A father's great disappointment, even for one day, with a birth of the girl, instead of son, after many years can lead to the daughter's repeated attempts at suicide. It can also be passed on to the grandchildren. The subconscious programs located in the child's energy field get transferred, with age, to the conscious mind, especially during puberty, and that brings conflict into the relationship between the child and the parents. Five minutes of denial can cost many years of rejection, blame, resentment and hatred. This is why adherence to ethical norms and spirituality is more important for good health than lotions and injections.

There is one more important peculiarity. The program of suicide can be triggered by any powerful external program aimed at changing a person's behavior. The organism reacts to external force with an unwillingness to live.

I researched whether an external program purposely placed in the subconscious can have a negative impact on a person, triggering side effects. It turned out it can. Any powerful program can produce resistance, expressed as a program of self-destruction.

"What about the aversion therapy against smoking and drinking?"- my assistant asked me.

I tested a few people who went through aversion therapy and found programs of suicide, which appeared in their energy field after treatment. A sluggish suicide program can manifest as anger and higher irritability, as well as the appearance of thoughts about suicide and other negative changes in the disposition and behavior of this person.

A woman came for advice on whether she should attend an accelerated English course.

"I have to go to the US, so I decided to take a course where they teach you under hypnosis. But after a few sessions I started to feel unwell. Could you please advise me if I should continue this course?"

I examined her energy field structure – the magnitude of distortion had reached its limit, this is a sign of a coming serious illness. I checked her energy field from before she started the course – the distortion was minimal. What could cause such a significant deformation of the woman's energy field? I continued examining and found the reason – a violation of the law of information, the programming of a person's subconscious.

When information is forcefully placed in the person's subconscious mind, it causes a deformation of the energy field structures. Over time this can manifest in the form of disease on the physical level. It is a well known fact that once there were attempts in Bulgaria to do TV training under hypnosis. Indeed, people learned a lot more information, however, in three-four years students started experiencing such symptoms as memory loss, a sharp decline in the immune system and other negative phenomena.

A young woman told me that she liked a young man, who had no interest in her, and she was planning on asking a psychic to help her. Recently she noticed some problems with her health.

I analyzed her energy field structures and found an amazing thing. The woman booked an appointment with the psychic, their energy fields connected and information was transmitted, so the psychic's subconscious already started influencing the young man, persuading him to meet the woman that was in love with him. Nobody knew about it on the conscious level, nothing had happened in the physical world apart from the woman's thoughts and desires, but the energy field structures began to interact. The process of charming the young man started, the process of introduction of this rigid program into his subconscious. This caused a distortion of the young man's energy field structures, and, because the charm was a foreign program in his energy field, it initiated a program of self-destruction.

The woman who loved the young man received the same distortions in her structures and began feeling ill. The psychic also had a significant distortion of her energy field structures.

One unethical act created a tragic situation, and nobody could see the cause.

Violence can only lead to more violence. I was asked about the patients of Kashpirovskij and my examination, unfortunately, once again confirmed this conclusion. Any rigid program, that is foreign to the person's inner convictions, placed under hypnosis or through suggestion can turn into a program of self-destruction.

There's no doubt that in our current situation it is difficult to pronounce that all kinds of human programming should be banned. We cannot abolish the old without creating the new. We are not talking about prohibiting all medication that has little effect and just aggravates the karma of humanity, or stopping the system of aversion therapy. Instead, we should put together all our efforts to gradually replace force, which our medicine seems to favour, with the natural development of human spirituality, rebuilding harmony of humanity with the world.

About a year ago I started researching whether it was possible to eliminate person's addiction to alcohol naturally. I was asked to help a very smart and talented person who couldn't stop drinking and was on the verge of chronic alcoholism. He didn't believe that anybody could help him.

When I met him I said:

"Do you know why you are drinking? A human being has to love the surrounding world, and if he doesn't feel love, a state of discomfort starts to develop, the beginnings of spiritual suffering. A person tries to muffle the spiritual pain in various ways. This leads to drug addiction, alcoholism and various types of substance abuse. The true reason for drug addiction and alcohol abuse is a low level of love in the soul. This condition would appear as the result of strong resentment, because of the suppression of love to other people.

I listed the events where love was demolished in his life as well as those of his parents.

The powerful energy field deformation disappeared after correction. A few days later I checked his energy field again and it was clear, his craving for alcohol had disappeared. I checked him again in half a year: he had stopped drinking and completely recovered from his illness.

There was an interesting case that happened in Yalta. After my lecture a man came up to me with the following story. His neighbor had gotten into heavy drinking and couldn't get out of it.

"I decided to use your method and asked him: "Tell me, what happened to you before you got into drinking? What do you remember?". "Yes, potatoes were distributed to others and I didn't get any, I was very upset". He asked God to forgive his resentment and stopped drinking.

That was a funny situation, but it gives you a clear idea about what a person should do to get rid of similar addictions. First of all you have to stop being upset with the surrounding world, gain harmony with it, love it.

Harmony is love. The past, present and future – these are all objects of love. A person should strive to feel love in his soul and then he will have no reason for drinking.

The situation in the world today reflects the current spiritual level of humanity. More and more money is spent on drugs and the fight against them, but the results are paltry and drugs are overtaking a larger and larger territory. This results from a lack of understating - we shouldn't fight against drugs, but, instead, against the reason leading to the need for them. The reason is a low level of internal love in humanity.

"Because iniquity will be multiplied, the love of many will grow cold" – it was said of us two thousand years ago. Denying love to God and Divine feelings, denying love to parents and children, to oneself and to loved ones, to inanimate nature and the surrounding world – has become a habit in our lives. All these violations activate the program of the destruction of love and, as a result, an avalanche-like rise in cruelty that is impossible to cool, neither with alcohol nor with drugs. In order to get out of the current crisis and get rid of injuries, people must learn how to love - God, each other, the Universe, the surrounding world, their past, present and future. "God is Love". Some people think that this is the easiest thing… one must just say "I love" and feel love as a result. But love is a very complicated art, achievable only by constant hard effort.

Any cell in the body, to make its existence meaningful, should not only work constantly, but also obey the laws of unity with the entire organism. A human being is a cell of the Universe and his task is not only to perform his function properly, but also to strive constantly for contact and oneness with the Universe, for love towards God. Our contact with the Divine is conditioned not only by our desire and trust, but also by the purity of our spirit and body. We all have contact with the Divine, but the degree of it varies - the more pure the person the better the contact.

My six year old son came to me and said that his leg was sore.

"Do you know who God is? Place your hands on your knee and ask him to forgive your dad - he didn't want to live when he was eighteen, that's why you have a sore leg."

He asked and I could see his energy field recovering.

Not long ago I explained to my patient that retribution for resentment can catch up with adults, that the child is protected until he is thirteen-fifteen years old, his resentment has no effect on his karma, and only after puberty does he become responsible for his actions and violations. However, in recent years the energy of the Earth has changed dramatically. These days not only can seven and eight years olds attack and destroy each other energetically, even one-two year old children do this, just like adults.

I checked my daughter's energy field and found an evil eye on her from a blonde male. Aged - ten years old, her classmate. What is going to happen to our children when they grow up? After all, we destroyed the barriers of protection, and our children have inherited distorted energy field structures. What kind of diseases await them? What is going to happen to their psyches and to their children, if they have already started energetically attacking each other?

Often when I say: "You were suppressing your love for another person" to people they would answer: "But I didn't even love him". Every time I have to explain that love is an enormous feeling, which we have to carry through our lives and which has to extend to the entire world. This is love towards the whole organism we call the Universe. The main commandments from the Bible are the laws of the spiritual world, of the energy interaction between people. When a mother today destroys her children with words, looks, gestures, not to mention actions, she doesn't understand that she gives her child a program that in a year or two might push him under a car or cause serious illness.

If parts of one system start to compete with each other and stop paying attention to the center, the system falls apart. When love disappears from a person's feelings and gets replaced with another emotion, the protection is broken and negative feelings receive the green light for destruction.

I remember one parable. A monk came to a woman and asked: "Could you please let me stay in your place over night?" "I will let you stay if you do one of the following: kill the goat, make love to me, or have something to drink. Your choice." The monk thought to himself: "I can't knife the goat – that would be killing; I can't make love to this woman – that would be blasphemy; I guess I will have some wine – this will be the smallest sin of all." So he had some wine and after that he fulfilled all of the woman's other requests.

Love is the main structure, and if it's intact, then other violations won't yield catastrophic results. People get used to thinking that love is an emotion, that they are free to use it according to their wishes. This is an incorrect interpretation.

Love is something that we are part of. It embraces the entire world. Love and life are given to us, and we have no right to destroy them. When we are conquered by the emotions of petty property-owners, we start to kill the love in ourselves, we also destroy the highest spiritual structures that connect us with the Universe - we start managing something that doesn't belong to us.

The Seventh Reason

We have become very ignorant during the last decades of our history. We don't even understand the most basic things. Can many of us even give the right answer to the question: "What is food?"

Food primarily influences our energy field structures, and depending on what kind of influence you receive, this is what you become. I tested what happens with a person's energy when he eats, and, to my great surprise, discovered that people accept food through their first chakra. Proper nutrition can heal a man. Incorrect nutrition can bring no less harm than an incorrect worldview and bad behavior.

"And God said, Behold, I have given you every herb yielding seed, which is upon the face of all the earth, and every tree, in which is the fruit of a tree yielding seed; to you it shall be for food." According to the Bhagavad-Gita it is prohibited to eat food that was cooked more than three hours before: this is "dirty" food, because it is suitable only for the body, but it has nothing for the spirit.

There is a term In Judaism - "non-kosher meat". This is meat that contains blood. Under no circumstances, is this meat to be eaten. Why? Blood is the storage of data about the life of the physical body, it contains all the information about its diseases, feelings, and also about the emotion the animal experienced while been slaughtered.

One day a woman asked me to analyze the reasons for the strange behavior of the seven year old son of her relatives. The child smoked, was very attracted to alcohol and was even trying to flirt with older women. There was nothing child-like in this kid, his behavior was incredibly strapped down to the earth in its worst form.

I examined the reasons. All his spiritual parameters were extremely low, it could be said that "the devil lives in him". This was his father's fault, but it wasn't karmic, it was all about his life style. The parameters of his father's thinking, behavior and diet were all very low. It is difficult to imagine how a person must live in order to obtain such negative parameters – what could he have done to demolish the energy field of the child so completely?

"What does the boy's father do for living?" – I asked the woman.

"He lives in the village working as a butcher, he slaughters pigs.

I checked the level of subconscious aggression in the child - it was zero. This meant that his father didn't put emotion into his work.

"But he likes to drink the blood of animals" the woman said.

That clarified things. The energy field structure of the father, of this boy, received information about what the animals felt during slaughter through the animal's blood.

Our ancestors were much better educated than us. They prayed before killing animals, asked the animal to forgive them that they have to use it for food. By doing so they blocked all the negative consequences, which today we swallow without any thought.

I never understood the reason for the unspoken rule that prohibits reading while eating. It turns out that eating accompanied by reading a book, watching TV, or discussing political or family problems can traumatize a person's soul, because information has free access to the subconscious while eating. This is the basis for the ceremony of receiving communion, meaning "union with the Divine". If the priest thinks about his daily business during the ceremony, communion is not going to happen.

Every person has a soul, a holy origin. He also has human and animal beginnings. Under normal circumstances the body has to receive food from the soul, the soul – from the spirit, the spirit – from God[1]. It is unacceptable to eliminate any part of this sequence. A life, built only on the primitive principle of saturating the body with food, without caring about the rest, is a successful means of regression.

---

[1] Later the author changes his vision of relationship between such terms as body, spirit and soul.

Chapter 4

Technical Diagnostics

Currently there is considerable evidence that successful forecasting of future events, of living and inanimate objects' behavior is possible. It is relatively simple to deal with living objects. Their behavior can be analyzed, generalized, and it's possible to make a reasonably accurate forecast. For inanimate objects, this method is not suitable, because in the physical world, at first glance, they have no behavior, no program of realization of structural changes, no development in time and space. It is easy to predict the behavior of a person we know and very difficult to forecast the weather that will come in a month. In the current time frame the condition of an inanimate object is the result of the physical influence of other objects – it is formed from the interaction between the energy fields of an individual object with other objects. The genetic programs of living objects are only different from behavioral programs of inanimate objects when one considers the time parameter - when the time interval is large enough, the differences disappear.

If we analyze the evolution of living objects on Earth we can see an increasing rate of program implementation and differentiation of objects in time – that is, individualization, detachment from the surrounding world when the unity of energy fields increases. The main programs that are responsible for the physical state of living and inanimate objects are the information-energy structures. Analyzing them enables quite accurate forecasts.

Any living and inanimate object has two bodies: physical and temporal. The temporal body is realized in the physical and is formed by an information-energy field, therefore, it is possible to talk about the presence of information programs that exist in inanimate objects and also about the interaction between energy fields and genetic programs of living objects.

136

By influencing information-energy structures it is possible to change the physical condition and behavior of any object, and also examine its future. Telekinesis, diagnosis from a distance and the correction of the energy fields of living and inanimate objects, are all subject to the mechanism described above. So then, the information program is realized on the physical level, but the reverse mechanism should also exist - this is a necessary condition for the existence of the Universe. Any object can become an energy field structure, and then return to its initial state. An electron is a particle and a wave at the same time. A wave can transform into a particle, and a particle – into a wave. Hence, any object can be transformed to the level of information-energy fields, transferred to any spot in the Universe (because there is no space in the information fields) and later once again realized on the physical level. This is the principle underlying teleportation, or impacting remote objects, such as clouds.

Since the earth's climate, geochemical and tectonic features, are determined by information-energy processes, it's possible that direct human willpower can influence events and objects of the surrounding world.

The upcoming period of cataclysms is evidence of not only ecological change, but also points to the deformation of the information-energy structures of the Earth. Currently, any person trying to control the weather or influence inanimate objects, makes a negative impact on the system of energy field self-regulation of the biogenosphere and deforms the information-energy structures of the Earth. My examination shows that even simple dissatisfaction with the weather has a negative impact on energy field structures.

A high accuracy of diagnostics and multiple analyses of the possible consequences of influence must lie at the heart of any research on living and inanimate objects.

Traditional methods of technical diagnostics tend to focus on the detection of defects that already exist, that for some reason are hidden from the observer or inaccessible by equipment. Examining the energy field structures enables forecasting of future physical deformations of objects, because a series of events on the physical level is laid out in programs on the energy field level. Analysis of different levels of the energy field programs ensures the high accuracy of forecasting. However, since diagnosis is always an invasive interaction with the energy field of the object, then, if the operator has programs of destruction or self-destruction, they can be passed on to the energy field of the inanimate object and create conditions for its destruction. In this case the mechanism of energy field self-regulation initiates the reciprocal program destroying the operator. Therefore, influencing inanimate objects through information-energy structures can be dangerous for humanity, - as we are all united on the subtle level.

In the area of technical diagnostics the ethics of the operator, the purity of his subconscious karmic structures are just as important as the purity of a healer working with people. A high level of subconscious aggression in the information structures of humanity can cause a series of global man-made catastrophes in the near future, which are impossible to prevent by increasing the technical quality of staff (such as in Chernobyl). The question about the ecology of spirit is paramount, because spirit in particular determines the condition of the surrounding world.

The first time I used extrasensory testing to diagnose inanimate objects was in the spring of 1991 in Yalta. I decided to examine the effectiveness of testing in a new area. I was asked to find places on the map of the Crimean Peninsula that would be most favorable for vineyards. I checked the map with the dowsing rod. All the best places were located along the seashore and an agronomist who was a part of our group confirmed it. The most favorable areas for growing apples were in the center of the peninsula, according to my information, far away from the shore -- this information was confirmed as well.

Then I began looking for the most suitable places for habitation, places with high quality air and water. Also I checked the best places to build resorts and checked the types of diseases that could be cured by the conditions in these areas. The results were very interesting. All buildings built before the revolution of 1917, especially the mansions, were located in areas exceptionally favorable for the health and destiny of people. On the other hand, many new buildings were located in nonsuitable areas. Perhaps, in earlier times, city planners had intuitive feelings of where they should build. Cemeteries, parks and cultural places were located in the less favorable areas, whereas the areas where people lived permanently were usually more comfortable from the biofield perspective.

I tried to find a place on the map where the number of diseases would be the highest, including cancer, and such a place existed. These studies suggest that the Earth's surface is heterogeneous for human habitation: some zones are favorable and some are unfavorable. In addition, these zones are not related to any geochemical or geotectonic formations. This mechanism is not clear to me so far, but it exists and has an impact on people's lives.

In Crimea the favorable areas appear as spots on a map, but in St. Petersburg the story is completely different.

In 1991 I was approached by a professor from the Polytechnic Institute. He was interested in my method and he suggested using it for technical diagnostics. He was researching the ecology of the region and wanted to hold a series of experiments, to determine whether it was possible to use extrasensory studies to ascertain the condition of water basins. Similar studies have been conducted in the past - for example, it is possible to determine the presence of minerals, not only by flying over areas on an airplane, or as Uri Geller did, but also by examining the area using photos or maps.

We found detailed maps of the region and began our work. We examined the Neva River – the degree of pollution by phosphorus. I had thought that the highest concentration should be in the river's mouth, but it turned out that it was in the upper section of the Neva. The same result happened with nitrogen. The reason for this was careless agricultural work in the upper section of the Neva River, where phosphorus and nitrogen were getting washed off from the fields. There was a place in the river-bed where the level of pollution by phosphorus and nitrogen fell to zero - it was a band of absolutely clear water and this band was perpendicular to the river flow. These areas of clean water were known to the specialists, but no explanation existed for them yet. There were a number of observations by scientists from abroad of "the effect of clean water" in the areas, where, by all estimates, pollution should be highest.

After that I examined the river banks. The areas where Neva's water was considered clean were part of the ring of the most preferable regions for living. There is a very specific formation in the energy structure of St. Petersburg, which sustains clean water in the waterways and beneficially influences people living in the area. However, there are some areas that are less suitable for living, - they also have ring structures. In St Petersburg, unlike any other area, the existence of powerful, interconnected ring energy structures was discovered.

Today these studies can be useful not only for the construction of residential areas, but also for planning the location of high risk technical objects.

The next step was dedicated to the study of Lake Ladoga.

The stain of nitrogen pollution had the shape of a long pointed tongue, whereas the phosphorus pollution was shaped like a blot in the center of the lake.

"The "tongue" that you drew," professor said, "is absolutely correct -- the river Volkhov is bringing it. An industrial complex producing protein concentrates and many state farms are located on its banks. Indeed, Volkhov brings a huge amount of nitrogen. Saying that, I'd though that phosphorus should also have a "tongue" shape."

I checked again – there was a stain in the center of the lake again.

We put together a program that included two months of data processing work. Something, that took me two-three hours of work, requires a few months of work under ordinary circumstances. At the time when we worked on our map study to identify the phosphorus pollution, no other research been conducted yet. Later when the research vessels entered lake Ladoga, their results confirmed that the maximum phosphorus contamination was, indeed, located in the area I'd pointed out earlier. I couldn't read this information from anybody because the institute staff had no data at that time - I worked only with information. There was an 80% overlap between my findings and the data that had been collected.

Very interesting results were obtained while detecting the locations of water leaks in the "Octiabrskij" concert hall. I asked for the blueprint of the building and found places where the leaks should be. Some areas I'd pointed out were already being restored, some troubled spots I discovered before they started leaking. I was asked where the water was coming from – from the outside or from inside the building. I could feel that the water was coming from outside, from a pipe located a few dozen meters from the concert hall. Examining the pipes I could see clearly how the water flows, the condition of the pipes, I physically felt the behavior of the water in the places where the pipes branched out. It was even possible to determine which metals were present in the water.

This was a new discovery for me. I realized how easy it is for a person that masters the method of extrasensory testing, to switch from medical to technical diagnosis.

During a discussion of the diagnostic results I explained that there was nothing mystical about the potential of the method, that it was a manifestation of laws that are not yet acknowledged or understood by many.

The main characteristic of extrasensory diagnosis lies in the fact that I work not with physical objects, but with their energy fields, and the energy field contains much more complete and accurate information than the physical object itself.

"That means that it was possible to determine, in advance, what would happen at Chernobyl?" – I was asked.

"Testing shows that deformations of the energy field structures, which later led to the accident, appeared in the energy field of Chernobyl's nuclear reactor two years before the accident."

"Is it realistic to foresee the possibility of accidents at nuclear power plants?"

"Yes, but I can't check every nuclear power plant because my karma is not clean enough to do so. I have been intensely working on changing myself for over a year, however, my internal subconscious level of ethics is still not high enough."

During the diagnosis of any object it is necessary to connect with it on the energy field level. If curious people, interested in extrasensory work, try to diagnose nuclear power plants and suddenly go bald, it shouldn't surprise them. However this is not the most important thing.

Due to the fact that information-energy fields are heterogeneous and have different sublevels, if my karma isn't clean enough, the diagnosis of any object can inflict harm, disrupt the energy field structure of the diagnosed object, causing problematic outcomes.

The management of an organization asked me to test the professional competence of employees using their profiles. Bioenergetics allows, using pictures or handwriting, to determine not only the business qualities of a person, but also that of his health, destiny, and, in addition, all information related to his life.

I analyzed the staff and made some recommendations regarding their compatibility and ways to form a high quality group. The result was quite unexpected: shortly afterwards, the employees got so enthusiastic about their jobs that they stopped going home, spent nights at work, causing dissatisfaction among their wives and numerous family conflicts.

In another group, also formed on the basis of the results of their energy tests, the successful work and professionalism of the staff was way above the manager's capacity and they requested his dismissal.

The energy fields of living and inanimate objects have the same characteristics on the subtle level, interact among themselves, and thus any negative thought, emotion or act can impact an inanimate object and can harm it.

Since human information structures interact with the information structures of inanimate objects, destructive programs can be passed on from people to the energy fields of inanimate objects. For that reason, pilots, nuclear power plant operators and other specialists in the most critical lines of work, have to be kind on the inside, with negative values for their subconscious aggression parameters, otherwise, without even knowing it, they can cause emergencies.

A global increase of aggression in the subconscious structures of humanity impacts the Earth's energy and can create conditions for catastrophe.

All psychics and healers of the highest quality have very low levels of subconscious aggression, because, if they didn't it would be very dangerous to contact the information field of the Universe. An attempt to "multiply" psychics using accelerated methods without any consideration for their ethical parameters can lead to sad results.

A person's subconscious mind controls the entire Universe, but it exhibits the most control over the area of a sixty meter radius around the person – this is where the interaction and impact on all living and inanimate objects takes place. If some books are constantly close to a person, his subconscious mind can read the information from them. Very active reading of information happens while we sleep, therefore, it is dangerous to keep crime novels close to the head of a sleeping child.

The energy field of every living and inanimate object has information not only about the object itself, but also about what was happening around it. The energy field structure of any premises accumulates information, interacts with our energy fields and influences them. People who are arguing in the room have no idea that it affects the health of everybody present in the room now, and everyone who will be there later, because of the accumulation of negative energy by the information structures of the premises.

When a person emotionally destroys the energy field structure of an object, he receives a counter attack in return. The energy structure of a living object is just as autonomous as that of an inanimate object. The inanimate object can influence a living one, actively influencing and exchanging information with it.

Once after a few sessions with my patients, my watch stopped, despite the fact that it had been wound-up. I thought of Uri Geller, held the watch in my hand and it started working again. A startup mechanism exists, but how does it work? I began exploring the energy structure around my watch and found a high power disruption in the energy field. That means that our emotions can deform the energy field structure of inanimate objects and, thus, actively influence them.

Not long ago my assistant called saying that the TV in her parents' house was broken. Her father often watched different programs and would react very emotionally to economic and political events in the country. I tested the TV's energy field - it was distorted by a program of hatred.

My assistant told her dad:

"You have to understand that everything around you is alive - the TV, refrigerator, all of the items in the house. If you don't treat them nicely, they will respond in kind."

Her father was very surprised.

"Does this mean that I have such great abilities that I can even influence my TV?"

"Today everybody has great abilities. It's not to do with you in particular, but with everything happening on the Earth."

"What should we do now?"

"Think about the fact that the fault is yours and ask for forgiveness for the negative emotions that you experienced."

Half an hour later her father had fully comprehended the new information and the TV was working well again.

Our stuff, toiletries, clothes tend to accumulate information and retain it. If somebody were jealous, looking at something that belonged to me, his jealousy could leave a mark that would harm me if I were not protected by my inner kindness.

Once a lady approached me and asked me to help her find her gold chain. The chain was very beautiful, she liked it a lot, but it was unexpectedly lost and she didn't know where.

"I don't do these things," was my answer, "but you had to lose this chain, otherwise it would cause a lot of trouble. It contained a very powerful program of self-destruction, which could have been activated under certain circumstances."

The lady didn't believe me, but a week later she came back and told me with great surprise, that the chain had belonged to another woman before, who had tried to commit suicide when the city was under siege by the Germans during the Second World War. The chain wasn't even on her while that happed, just in the room, but information about this remote event was still stored in its energy field.

Once I consulted a woman with a rash. I couldn't find the reason at first, so I carried on a session to improve her overall condition. At the second session she mentioned that she didn't notice any changes in her health yet. I continued to search and found that the allergy was being triggered by plants and the disease manifested most at home. Any other place she felt just fine. I asked her to draw the plan of her apartment and detected that in the kitchen near the wall there was a place with the plants that were causing her disease. The woman confirmed that there were a few potted plants: aloe, tulips, and daffodils. I looked at their energy fields to find out what plants' attitudes were towards the woman. It turned out that all of them had a poor attitude. And the reason was that her mother didn't like plants while she was pregnant, nor did she like them after giving birth. This program entrenched itself in my patient's subconscious and now this woman, without any awareness, attacks plants - in return she receives attacks in kind.

Many allergic reactions – such as to plants, animals and fish – are caused by the fact that our ancestors had negative emotions towards these entities. These objects react to irritation and hatred towards them and this can become a cause for allergy. Negative emotions, experienced by ancestors a while ago or by a person in his past incarnations remain blocked until the person activates them by, for example, swearing at tiresome dust or at a fish that gave him food poisoning or at something else. There are numerous examples of how inanimate objects can influence people.

A woman was on vacation with her children and because of bad weather they had to spend most of their time in their room. The children watched TV, but she wanted to read the literature that had accumulated on her list. The TV programs disturbed and irritated her, bringing on a feeling of discontent. After coming back from vacation the woman's health sharply deteriorated and no one among traditional doctors could find a reason for her illness. It turned out that it was her dislike for the TV during those two weeks, it was an attack on an inanimate object on the energy field level.

I had another patient – she had numerous problems with her health and severely deformed energy field structures. I analyzed her problems – for over twenty years the women didn't like the copying equipment that she had to work with.

"Our equipment was old, something would constantly break down. I even didn't want to go to work because of this," – she explained.

A young woman in a bad mood angrily put her cigarette out on a car hood. She would never have guessed that this was the reason for her headaches - the program of hatred towards a particular item and this item's response in kind, because at the energy field level living and inanimate objects react the same way.

Any negative emotion towards an inanimate object can cause distortions of the energy field structures of a person. Think of a mother, who beats a table leg because her child just ran into it, saying: "Don't cry! You see, now it is in pain as well". Raising children this way doesn't teach them the proper way to act towards the world and creates future problems for the child.

I had a very difficult relationship with the PC I used while working on this book. One day I was getting ready to work and found that there was something wrong with my PC, there were some sort of distortions on the screen. I thought I could correct its energy field, so I connected to the computer's energy field, but I got a feeling of physical discomfort. I diagnosed the issue and found a deformation of the energy field structure in the chest area. This kind of distortion I usually see whenever I offend somebody.

Sometimes it is difficult for a reader to comprehend what I have to say, but I report only facts. To restore normal physical wellbeing I had to find who was upset with me and what I had done to offend them. A few minutes later I found who was resenting me. It was my PC, and I found the reason. There was a destructive program "sitting" in my energy field. Three years before I was born my father felt hatred towards a person, who had offended him. This destructive program, initiated in my father energy field, was passed on to me and realized not only as illnesses and traumas, but also in attacks on persons with whom I was in contact, including my children. My PC reacted acutely to this program – its energy field attacked me in response and broke through my energy field shell. After I eliminated this program from my energy field, the computer calmed down too.

I was interested in checking whether a machine can "treat" different people differently and I was amazed to see that, indeed, it didn't react the same way to the energy field of every operator. The machine reacted very negatively on operators with a negative karma, meaning that they had programs of destruction and self-destruction in their energy fields. It "didn't like" one of the computer operators the most, whose energy field was particularly harmful to the machine. That was the moment I began understanding the mechanism of a phenomenon noticed many years ago, that some people have a negative effect on equipment - it breaks down or stops working in their presence.

Once my acquaintance complained about pain in her kidney and asked me to find the cause. I started to examine her energy field structures.

It wasn't her who violated the laws of the Universe, it was an inanimate object from her apartment. I pointed out the place on the apartment's blueprint where this object should have been located. It turned out this was a place where icons were hung. Two icons were ancient, but the rest were painted on cardboard, bought in church. I checked how these icons regard the owner, whether there were any laws they might violate with respect to her. Two icons, depicting Jesus Christ and St. Nicolas were saturated with programs of hatred and destruction. That sounds blasphemous – a depiction of Jesus Christ was experiencing hatred and programmed the owner of this icon towards self-destruction. After a detailed examination of the first icon I discovered that the person who painted this icon, didn't want his child. A person with this sort of program in his energy field has no right to paint icons. The artist, who painted the St. Nicolas icon, throughout many years refused the feeling of love to his children and to his father, therefore, he also coded the icon's energy field with emotions refusing the Divine. This information helped the woman understand why, for a long time, she didn't like being in this room.

Many years ago not every artist would have access to the painting of icons. Intuitively, a person with pure karma would be chosen. But that wasn't enough, this person's karma had to be blocked from negative influences. This state could be achieved through personal ethics, aspiration for the Divine, and also by long fasting and prayers – the renunciation of material attachments. Icons used to be drawn only at moments of inspiration using paint, diluted with holy water. These kinds of icons can heal people. Just their presence would harmonize the energy field structures of a diseased person, moreover, not only would the body heal, but, most important, the soul. These kinds of icons in a room influence people's character, health and destiny in a positive way.

However icons that were drawn in a regular state of mind can harm people even after consecrating them in church. It's important to note that everything related to the name of Jesus Chris is allowed into our subconscious without hindrance. I checked how icons printed in a printing house affect people, and found that they are not perfect either. Only real icons or their photographs have a positive effect.

An interesting story happened to me once. I brought a radio to my studio and noticed that the quality of the sound got noticeably worse. I thought that the receiver was broken and brought it back home. However, at home it worked normally. So I took it again to my studio where it stopped working completely and this time for a long time. I tested what was happening and found that the radio had been negatively impacted by some other inanimate object in the studio. I got the blueprints of my studio and started my investigation. It was the icon that was about a meter away from the radio.

One day I was asked to diagnose a boy from one of the Baltic countries. The powerful deformation of his energy field and the related illness were caused by his father's violations two years before his birth. Some kind of blasphemy took place then and it was with regard to ceremonial objects. I asked the boy's mother if she could remember any events associated with icons or church items. She recalled that two years before their son was born her husband put an icon in a bar, where bottles of alcohol were stored. On the energy level it looked like blasphemy, hatred towards the inanimate item, the icon, and towards the Divine. Because this act was predetermined by the father's information-energy structure, the son, who inherited the same structures, had to work off his spiritual imperfection.

Any inanimate object, no matter how implausible it may sound, has its "personal" attitude towards other objects, including people. This is most noticeable in ceremonial objects and may explain the reason for the premature deaths of people of certain professions, who come in contact with these types of objects due to their job description, for example - archeologists, artists.

On the other hand, in churches today there is a very active trade in Christian literature, candles, icons and other religious artifacts. Why did the servants of Christianity forget: "And Jesus went into the temple of God, and cast out all those that sold and bought in the temple..."?

I tested what trade contributes to the energy of a church. From a house of prayer the church transforms into a house of trade. Apparently, for some reason priests can't feel it or can't oppose it, but the problem remains - trade destroys the energy of a church. Bioenergetic analysis shows that to restore the energy of the temples all trades should be taken outside their premises.

I heard an interesting story in Kronstadt, a town near St. Petersburg. There was a half-ruined church in the city, and the old residents remember when the authorities tried to blow it up. Explosives had been laid a few times, even the neighboring buildings had started to crack, but the church stayed and it was impossible to destroy it. The young officer in charge of the blasting operation, died shortly after. His wife didn't live much longer and their child was taken to an orphanage. Not long ago at the age of thirty the son unexpectedly passed away in his apartment without any serious disease or any visible reason. The family ceased to exist. A weird coincidence – his father was around his thirties when he detonated the church.

I analyzed what had happened to the family, why they all died. What was the reason for this particular sequence of events? I discovered the following: at the beginning the officer directed the blasting operation only as an executor, but later, when he saw that the church did not fall apart, he got emotionally involved - he put his soul into the work he performed. A clash with the egregor of the church happened, with the programs of love and unity. These programs also unite and oppose the aggressive programs - therefore, the officer's program of destruction was returned back at him. Since his wife and son were united with him on the energy field level, all of them died.

Hatred towards an individual, hatred towards a building, the desire to kill somebody, the desire to demolish a church, unhappiness with the surrounding world – all of these can lead to self-destruction, and, because everything is alive on the subtle level, any kind of aggression will lead to serious consequences. One American astronaut shared his feelings after flying to the Moon, saying that the whole Universe is a living creature - that our Earth is also alive and very intelligent.

A small digression. We walked around the city and close to Liteyskij Avenue found an unusual building that looked like a stalactite. Looking at this building I got a feeling of disharmony, something obtrusive, something associated with destruction. I examined how the building interacted with people, what kind of impact its facade was making. The result was quite interesting: the parameters of psyche and body were influenced in a very negative way, meaning that just observing the facade of this building caused certain deformations of human spiritual-energy field structures.

This is just additional confirmation of the fact that we lost our intuitive feeling of harmony and didn't gain a new understanding of the world - that is why we construct buildings that are harmful simply by the fact of their existence.

My research suggests that from June 1987 a substantial negative shift happened in the information-energy structures of the Earth, programs of destruction started to unite and activate. Therefore, currently, any negative thought or emotion, even an insignificant one, is amplified by the negative programs of the information field of the Earth. On the energy field level the separation of people into two camps is taking place: those who are striving for love and kindness and those who are experiencing a rapid process of spiritual degradation, due to the saturation of their bio-energy fields with negative programs.

Chapter 5

Culture, Art and the Karmic Structures of Human Beings

Everything that surrounds a person influences him: space, household items, books, movies, plays - because everything has an information-energy field and interacts with the energy fields of people.

Testing allows for determination of the extent and quality of this influence. If books, movies carry elements of aggression they can cause deformations of the energy field structures with consequences that are easy to predict.

Since August 1945 there has been an increase in subconscious aggression in the information structures of the Earth. Strategic resources of spirituality are now almost completely exhausted, and life adds new portions of aggression every day.

A particularly high level of aggression is in western mass art that is built on the principals of competition and the propoganda of violence. When an endless stream of videos flooded Russia and became uncontrollable, the process of their influence on our subconscious got out of control. Even harmless, at first glance, children's cartoons, in their majority contain programs of violence, and what makes it even more dangerous, these programs are packaged in a soft, elegant way. Information that stimulates positive emotions, gets into our subconscious freely, entrenches deeply and stays there for a long time, because the subconscious mind works autonomously and can accept information independently, without criticism.

To assess the influence of some Soviet and foreign movies on a person we are going to use basic parameters: the level of conscious and subconscious aggression. As it was mentioned before, the value for the parameter of subconscious aggression for any object should be negative. Talented works of art always carry the potential of humanism and have a very low level of subconscious aggression. For example, the poetry of A. S. Pushkin has a very low figure for subconscious aggression.

Let's go back to mass art. I tested the famous cartoon "Tom and Jerry": conscious aggression – zero, subconscious – plus eighty. Next is the children's classic "Snow White and the Seven Dwarfs": conscious aggression – minus forty, subconscious – plus sixty. These movies, despite their external kindness, place inner cruelty into the subconscious - after viewing them the level of a child's subconscious aggression increases a few times.

Today, unfortunately, children are held responsible for their own violations of the highest laws, and that means that disintegration will follow – of either of soul, or spirit, or body. When disintegration starts at the age of one or two this will lead to the degradation of the child's personality, so the child, in fact, will lack vitality. So why should we complicate and burden the lives of our children through damaging art?

Let's recall some movies that were on soviet TV and in the cinema not so long ago. The movie "Cinderella" has a conscious aggression of minus fifty, and subconscious – minus twenty; "The prisoner of the Caucasus" – minus one hundred sixty and minus one hundred respectively; the cartoon "Just you wait" – plus twenty and minus one hundred twenty; "White Sun of the Desert" – minus sixty and minus fifty; "Solaris" – zero and minus two hundred ten; "Andrei Rublev" – plus twenty and minus two hundred and forty.

This is what we lived with - this was Art.

Examining the level of subconscious aggression in different social groups, including politicians, popular singers, entertainers, I confirmed, once again, that the system of the energy field self-regulation works impeccably.

A person standing on a stage has a very powerful influence on the subconscious mind of listeners or viewers. Therefore, only a person with a minimal level of subconscious aggression and maximum level of fullness of love can contact and work with large audiences, otherwise the spiritual structures of people could be harmed greatly. All Russian stage, theater and movie stars have very low levels of subconscious aggression, there are no exceptions. Even a insignificant increase in the level of aggression leads to "rejection" by life: the person can lose his abilities, talents, unexpectedly get sick, leave the stage because of an accident or, by fate's will, his career will start to fall apart without any visible reason.

Therefore the highest level of professionalism for actors and singers must include not only professional qualities, but they should also be accompanied by inner kindness and fullness of love. It is necessary to develop these qualities in yourself and to work on them constantly. It might surprise you, but the same mechanism works in the sphere of politics. A politician with high subconscious aggression has no future, his will and intellect, in fact, are secondary.

Subconscious aggression is very dangerous for young people, especially pregnant women, because a mother's spirit becomes the child's body, and the deeper aggression, the more dangerous it becomes. A woman who doesn't oppose her inner aggression harms her own psyche only by two percent, but if a year or two later she has a baby, then the distortion of the baby's psyche can be as high as eighty percent, because the child's body is shaped by the mother's thoughts and emotions.

People always knew this. During the Renaissance, pregnant woman would be taken to art exhibitions, surrounded by beautiful things, music and love. In Russian villages people knew - what an expectant mother sees, feels and thinks has a high impact on the child and they tried to protect the woman, even from strangers' eyes. Now let's imagine our contemporary woman crowded in public transport, sworn at while standing in a que, who "relaxes" by watching the next movie from the west...

We have an extremely simplistic image of the mechanism of karma, we cannot always see the entire process of self-regulation as a whole. Today the hygiene of our ethics and spiritual life must not be empty words, but the result of a deep understanding of the world and its laws. The difficulty lies in the need to learn how to combine opposing terms: idealism and materialism, religion and science, logic and intuition, high spirituality and practicality; it is necessity to combine constant love towards the world and people with our everyday emotions.

In our time, the mutual influence of people on each other became an uncontrollable process, and art plays a significant role in this.

In the middle of the XIX century, starting with the development of impressionism and some other trends in art that were focused on the subconscious mind, it became increasingly difficult to protect the subconscious from penetration by aggression.

The majority of western painters have low spirituality and a high degree of subconscious aggression. Such paintings deform the biofield structures and, in fact, even harm people. Sometimes you can find paintings at exhibitions that even take their viewer's energy - after viewing these paintings a person feels tired and worn out, unaware of what happened.

A surprising discovery for me was the exhibition of the ritual paintings by Australian artists, which took place this spring. After testing several works of art I was surprised by the power of positive influence on the basic, most important human parameters: the fullness with love and connection to the Cosmos. I stopped in front of one of the paintings. It didn't have particular images, it all consisted of dots, lines and stains. Standing in front of it I could feel how it interacted with me. I decided to move closer and found myself in the painting's information field. This was a strange feeling - suddenly the scale changed, I felt spellbound and unreal. The parameters of the picture's impact were splendid: very high scores on spirituality, soulfullness and fullness of love, and extremely low parameters of conscious and subconscious aggression. This painting, without bringing any conscious association, would heal a person energetically, provide him with information, and interact with him as a living being.

After attending this exhibition I tried healing using images and was surprised by the power of their influence. It helped me understand the meaning of talismans, mandalas, icons. Having an active energy field structure they harmonize not only a person's spirit, health and destiny, but also the space around them. An icon, written by a spiritual artist, not only introduces a person to the Divine, but also heals and protects him. Contemporary paintings should be created as icons, because the main problem of today's world is a lack of spirituality.

Blind following of western trends in art just makes the economic disaster in Russia worse – by adding spiritual disintegration on top of it. It looks like the tremendous spiritual potential accumulated by Russia throughout decades of spiritual suffering is sinking into the sand. If before, paintings created here, from the energetic point of view, were like trees with powerful root systems and thick crowns, now they could only be compared to a pitiful tree growing in a swamp. All that is left is the trunk, representing technical execution.

Today's world lives mostly according to the ego's needs, but the feelings related to the ego are just the tip of the iceberg. And something that is not visible – love, connection to the Cosmos, spirituality - these are all simply discarded, because they don't provide immediate results.

Having created a few paintings oriented towards the subconscious mind, I discovered that a fundamentally new painting is possible, which can be a hundred times more powerful by influencing the spiritual world of a person. Accordingly, the demands on the painter, his spiritual world, are a hundred times greater as well. The attempts of a few painters to create a healing painting were meaningless because they were contemplating the healing of a human being as physical healing. The body depends too much on the condition of the spirit, therefore, only paintings full of love and spirit can have a healing effect.

Analyzing ways of spiritual development and the renewal of humanity, I tested several countries to identify the potential for their spiritual development. I have also tested the interaction between such concepts as "culture" and "civilization". The word "culture" comes from the world "cult". The cult's artefacts and cult itself are focused on something that unites everybody, something super-material. Hence, culture emerges as a result of striving for unity, for the Divine as the ultimate symbol of unity. Only after unity is formed, is dissociation, materialization, that which we call "civilization", possible. Culture defines a continuous spiritual renewal of a nation; civilization works for physical renewal. Culture creates civilization, but at certain point civilization begins to reject and demolish culture.

In order for the development process to be continuous, the accumulation of spiritual values is necessary. Structures opposing an exclusive focus on physical, material wellbeing must exist in society – structures that would prepare the potential for cultural renewal. Nowadays, because faith has been weakened, there is very little potential for spiritual renewal, therefore, the issue is even more relevant.

It is interesting to look at the very notions of "culture" and "civilization" from the point of view of bioenergetics. "Culture" is characterized by the following parameters: conscious aggression – plus ten, subconscious - minus two hundred ten; the concept of "civilization": conscious aggression – minus fifty, subconscious – plus fifty. This just proves that culture is aiming at creation, and civilization carries elements of destruction.

I tested some countries to determine their potential for developing culture and civilization; the evaluation was based on the parameter of aggression only. Germany: conscious aggression – minus fifty, subconscious – plus fifty, USA: conscious – zero, subconscious – plus two hundred; Japan: conscious– minus forty, subconscious – minus ten; Russia: conscious– plus one hundred eighty, subconscious – minus two hundred ten.

Analyzing these numbers we can conclude that Germany is the country, ideally corresponding to the concept of civilization; America – the country of highest civilization, but also its further development will require a lot of work to reduce the level of subconscious aggression; Japan reconciles culture and civilization and preserves potential for future development; Russia, at the moment, has no civilization, but it has inner culture and colossal potential. This clarified, for me, the meaning of prophecies by many clairvoyants claiming that salvation will come from Russia.

Chapter 6

What Is Diabolism

It is tragic that people don't understand that truth is not constant and changes with time; this can be observed everywhere. The perception of truth that existed, let's say, five thousand years ago and presently are quite different. Changes in the world can occur at different speeds and it requires continuous reflection. Lack of understanding of the laws of the world and their violations leads to energy field deformation and disintegration, creates powerful negative programs that live independently in the information-energy field structures of human beings.

Many world religions have a term called "diabolism". This concept can be studied and analyzed energetically using extrasensory testing.

We already know that human thoughts, reaching the subconscious, create an information field which contains an enormous number of stand-alone programs, both positive and negative. Programs of destruction exist in the information field as independent organisms, subordinate to specific laws.

How did I discover these programs of destruction and start to working with them? The research and analysis of energy field structures shows that there are large masses of powerful independent programs of self-destruction present in the information fields of both individuals and humanity as a whole, created by people over many years. These programs work as disease, they can independently move from the energy field of one person to another and can even be supported by the central block of the programs of humanity, because at the level of collective consciousness we are all united.

These programs are neutral as long as there are no conditions for their activation. As soon as a person adds negative emotions or throughout the course of treatment it becomes necessary to eliminate these programs, they become activated very quickly, and this happens in a quite peculiar way – they start working on subtle information structures. People don't have organs that control these processes, therefore everything happens unnoticeably for a person.

You can call it a disease caused by a "virus". The "virus" of destruction starts working actively, initiating programs of the person's destruction. When an organism violates the highest laws, moves away from the evolutionary path of development, its energy structure is deformed, its protection is penetrated and it becomes easy pickings for the "virus", which takes on the function of a punishment system. The punishment looks quite odd – the "infections" and "viruses" start to multiply and form new structures. Humanity, having started to deviate from the correct path (and the correct path is the unity with the Universe), is punished by the activation of negative programs, multiplying on the highest spiritual structures and demolishing them.

Since the body and spirit are a united information-energy system, the "infection" first destroys a person's soul at the spiritual structure level, and afterwards goes on to destroy the body. Programs of self-destruction can consolidate and exist as independent structures, staying for decades in the humanity's common energy field they try to infiltrate an individual's psyche and soul, so that the person activates them by his behavior. Programs start to behave as typical viruses, which first enter a single cell and start multiplying vigorously, eventually destroying the entire organism.

An information virus on the energy field level of humanity is apparently the devil that the Bible talks about. If a person doesn't take the path of spiritual development, if he starts to refuse the laws of development of the Universe, he inevitably becomes pray for such a "virus", which is always waiting for our mistakes.

I myself experienced how this "virus" acts and how it starts to develop. I have to admit that it was quite a dangerous exercise, because any mistake on my part could have brought about dramatic results not only for me, but also for the group of people that worked with me. The starting point was, when analyzing the energy field structures of different diseases, I noticed that starting from 1987 almost all of my patients had had their negative programs activated. After 1987 the deformations of energy field structures increased considerably in size, and presently the punishment for delinquencies have become much harsher.

What does that mean – a stronger punishment? If a person does something negative towards himself or towards somebody else, then his act is powered and activated by his energy field – through the intensification of his negative emotions. Any negativity can be accumulated in a person's energy field and amplified tenfold.

The impact of all negative emotions increased sharply. Since a thought is an information unit, then all positive and negative thoughts group into structures, and later, into information systems.

During the last six years, the structures of the information fields of human beings have been activated - these structures aim for destruction, not survival. Moreover, these structures have very interesting behavior. First of all, they seek to destroy the primary spiritual structures, which block the physical disintegration of an organism. If a person is ethically educated and strives to retain his spirituality, then the impact will be directed at his body. The person will start getting sick more often. We think about serious diseases as something negative, but this is a very superficial perception. By restraining our body, the disease protects our spiritual structures from disintegration. This is a different story than when a disease is the result of the destruction of spiritual structures, resulting in physical disintegration.

What follows is the first case where I personally experienced a program of destruction.

I was analyzing the reason behind why a young man, kind and gentle, suddenly expressed powerful aggression towards his friends. An examination of the causes showed that his behavior was largely determined by his father. There was a program of destruction in the father's energy field; his father activated the program and the son executed it, manifesting it in his behavior.

I examined the case, finished my work and an hour later, while walking around the city, I suddenly felt an incomprehensible energy attack. It seemed as if somebody took a stick and stirred my brain in my head, everything swam in front of my eyes and an incredible weakness overtook me. Physically I felt as if I was "spun" in the washing machine. My condition was worsening by the minute. Then I felt that I couldn't walk, so I had to sit down on a bench and take a fifteen minute nap. When I woke up I still didn't feel well, I moved as if I were submerged in oil. It was very difficult to walk, I felt a real heaviness on my back, as if someone was hanging on me.

My condition was due to an energy attack from the father of the young man. While diagnosing my patient, I connected with the energy field of his father and he started to attack me quite professionally despite the fact that he had no idea of it – it was the charge aimed at destruction that lay in his subconscious and it worked quite actively. The autonomous program of destruction, existing in the energy field of the young man's father, could act not only against himself and his son, but also against other people - actual work on the physical level.

I had no choice, but to influence this aggressive structure. Because the structures of destruction feed on violations of the laws towards people – such as harming people, destroying love – I examined all of the violations, committed by the father and by his ancestors, and made the necessary corrections. Only after that did the attacks end. This event confirmed to me that, when contacting any negative program, there is strong aggression possible not only at the information level, but at the energy level as well.

What is evil? The same act in different circumstances may have different meanings. From the perspective of the karmic mechanism, evil is destruction, and good is creation. On the other hand, the development of the new is always happening through the destruction of previous structures, but the destruction in creation must be controlled. Thus evil is uncontrolled good.

If a spiritual beginning lies in the basis of destruction, then destruction is creation; however, when the spiritual is exhausted, destroying becomes uncontrollable.

Therefore, civilizations that used up all their spirituality, destroy everything, including themselves.

While watching TV I heard the phrase: "Evil has never been so sexual" - this was an advertisement for the next American movie. What does it mean? The information, received through the first chakra is neither controlled, nor restrained by anything. If aggression moves down to the first chakra then the system of self-regulation blocks it in the forms of feminine infertility and death or serious illness for her children. This mechanism works slowly, sometimes stretching over several generations. Now the pace of all processes, the rhythm of life, the degree of human influence has increased so much that sometimes the system of self-regulation can't keep up with these changes and, therefore, an accumulation of aggression takes place in the hereditary information structures.

In world art recently, and especially in American art, an increasing multiplication of violence is very noticeable. Especially during the last few years the tendency of converging violence and sex has been outlined. What happens to a person who watches movies promoting violence? His external aggression moves into the subconscious and becomes uncontrollable.

Not long ago I had to do an interesting diagnosis. It concerned a dog with a very high level of aggression. Somebody suggested to the owner to drug the dog. After that the aggression in the dog's behavior disappeared and for a long time it was a kind, quiet dog.

However, a few months later the dog had puppies, and .... she ate them. The owner had to put her down.

I analyzed what happened there. The dog had a powerful center of aggression in its head area, which was formed by the high level of conscious aggression of its owner.

After taking a drug the aggression moved to the dog's first chakra, therefore the puppies were born with a very high level of aggression, which was "multiplying" very quickly in their energy field. The chain of the aggression "multiplication" was interrupted, but its source remained.

I was healing one patient, then another, then a third and discovered a substantial intensification of all negative programs. This is evidence that the ecology of the spirit of humanity is not well - an aggressive program exists in the energy field of humanity and this program manifests as violations of the highest laws by people.

I decided to check whether humanity, as a whole, commits any violations of the highest laws. As soon as I tried to reach this level I was powerfully attacked. I started to search for the person attacking me. Usually I can find the person, examine his energy field structures from a distance, make a correction - and in this way eliminate the attack. This time, there wasn't a particular person, I was facing the general program of aggression directly.

When I attempted to examine the situation from the point of view of humanity, hoping to help it, I encountered frantic resistance, the central negative program began the attack. This central negative program is what I call the devil. I tested the parameters of this program: conscious aggression – minus two hundred ten, subconscious – plus two hundred ten. This means that our conscious mind can't register this program, it is completely imperceptible, and most aggressive at the subconscious level.

I noticed the fact that a disease can resist healing. In this case, shamans would say: "We need to banish the evil spirit". From the energy point of view, this evil spirit is the program of destruction. Any person, by violating the highest laws, initiates the program of destruction in his energy field, taking place at different levels, including the physical. A shaman has subconscious information about it and can straighten the energy field structure of the person, but he won't necessarily provide knowledge regarding correct behavior. When sorcerers and magicians tell the person that he didn't behave properly and that's why the evil spirits settled in him, they emphasize the close relationship between the person's health and his observance of the laws of ethics.

When I begin to work on the subtle levels and find disease, it behaves like a living creature, it starts actively resisting and attacking me. I defend myself against it, and a "duel" between the healer and the disease takes place. I suppose many healers of the highest level can feel it. A disease is not just a "clump of dirt" that you can take and throw away, it's a living organism, which can be very aggressive. If the healer can't find the cause and starts healing incorrectly, then he either won't heal the patient or will take the disease upon himself – he will receive the negative subconscious mind set or the program of destruction that had caused the disease in his patient.

I have to say that the spiritual disease of humanity – diabolism – acts much more creatively than physical disease. At the physical level programs are much more sluggish, while at the subtle level – they are quick, aggressive and act with virtuosity, they can even place the program of self-destruction in a person's subconscious. Any person attempting to fight the negative program receives a supply of destruction from it, which works to destroy him as an information system. When my team tried to work with this program using energy we faced a powerful attack from it. There was a feeling as if something had been lowered down on us, gently, but surely, as if everything was being taken softly out of our bodies.

The resistance of negative programs can manifest in different ways. The next example confirms how strong, dangerous and unexpected these manifestations can be.

I was talking to a reporter for the journal on bio-energetics, and the subject turned to diabolism. Scepticism in my attitude with-respect to this question had been shaken already. The church believes that an enormous amount of unmotivated suicides occur in our time because the devil influences them. Should I translate this into the language of bio-energetics, this can be taken to mean that, negative programs accumulated by humanity, mature and activate in people with the constant activation of ideas of violence incite people to all kinds of unmotivated behaviors. I was explaining this mechanism to the reporter and said a few unnecessary phrases ...

The point here is that ethics should be adhered to in everything, including the usage of information. These few phrases, from my point of view, could be harmful for an unprepared reader, because some of the information was still difficult to comprehend. When I realized this I suggested we erase the two-minute recording. We rewound the tape and started erasing. Everything was erased, but the key phrase. We repeatedly erased – and again the phrase we wanted to delete remained , and, in addition, it "floated", moving throughout the tape. We wiped about ten minutes of recorded time, but we still couldn't remove that phrase. That was a strange feeling. It was the first time I'd seen something like that. Finally, only after influencing it energetically, we managed to delete the phrase.

Examining this occasion later I found that there was a program of destruction in my energy field and it stubbornly resisted – it was resistant to removal on the physical level. This fact might resemble fiction, but this happened to me in reality. That means that the danger of what is called diabolism is inside a person, and not outside.

The program of destruction can be in anybody's energy field, including the most kind, most accommodating, most ethical person; it is difficult to detect by regular means. It develops and, similar to a virus, captures the subtle structures, the soul, disfigures and deforms it. In fact, these days, the program of destruction of humanity has been launched.

The energy capacity of spirit and soul in a human being is large. Having committed an improper act a person can physically feel perfect. The diseases can start a few years later, but the spiritual disintegration condemns the person's children and grandchildren to health issues. A person that has committed an unseemly act does not feel and does not understand that once initiated, the program of destruction will unwind in his energy field autonomously.

The subconscious mind today is incredibly aggressive. I realized this relatively recently and started to look for the reasons. It turned out that if before, aggression fed off cruelty at behavioral level, nowadays it feeds off small, barely noticeable to the first glance, details of our lives. For example, it could be a house with disharmonious architecture, a cartoon like "Tom and Jerry", with high subconscious aggression, a pin cushion in the shape of a man (where one sticks needles). These all are elements of aggression, the realization of programs of humanity's self-destruction.

Professional qualities, intellect, skills are not the most important things in a person. Only taking care of the improvement of professional skills, absence of striving for spiritual development can lead to a "rejection" by fate. An attempt to advance skills without understanding the laws of the universe and without the development of ethics is especially suicidal in the field of bioenergetics. This trend leads to our children having greater and greater energy potential and less and less energy for the proper use of it. The power goes out of control and the simple decision: "tomorrow I will be kind" is not going curb it. I know a young man, who had to discover for himself what it meant to have power without ethics.

Once a group of psychics, including me, were diagnosing the sailors on a ship that was on a regular trip. During the break I was approached by a man and asked to help his son. I agreed and a young man around twenty two years old entered the room with an apathetic face and lifeless look. This young man had undergone insulin shock treatment a few times, but his condition remained the same, and most important – the reason for it was unknown to the doctors. I asked him to tell me about himself.

"When I was a child I noticed that I could predict some events, and I tried to practice and develop these skills. While I was serving in the army my ability to influence improved dramatically, I could read people's minds, influence their will.

"While I was standing guard," – the young man said. "I could see people who tried to climb over the fence in the wrong place. I would send a mental order to these people to fall off the fence and they did. Or, I remember once there was a man walking in front of me with a shopping bag of empty dishes. Mentally I ordered this man – 'Fall down!' – and immediately he fell and broke all the dishes. I also noticed that before people even asked their questions I would start answering them. I could even just look at a cloud and it would 'clear up'".

I checked the parameters of aggression in the young man – they had reached the maximum value, almost all his energy was aimed at destruction.

In the meantime the young man continued his story:

"Gradually I started noticing that all my abilities were always aimed at causing harm and destruction. I was advised to go to church and get baptized. During the baptizm, when I was walking through the altar I felt as if something inside me snapped and I felt an incredible sadness and sorrow. For a few days I was in a terrible state and then I went to see the priest who had baptized me and told him that I was dying. The priest advised me to place the Bible under my pillow at night. I felt even worse in the morning, as if somebody had placed a weight on my head. If I started praying as the priest suggested, all the windows and doors in the room would open and rain would start pouring outside. After a few months of this torment I was admitted to a psychiatric hospital."

"Is it possible to help my son?" – the young man's dad asked me.

I took him into another room and explained that the cause of the problem lay in them, the parents.

"Can your wife get here?"

"Certainly, she can be here in two days."

So later I spoke to the tired, exhausted woman, the young man's mother.

"Your son's problems are mostly determined by your incorrect orientation, by a distorted worldview. Your son can be called a black magician. From the paternal side he received great energy abilities, and from you – hatred towards people. Why did you hate your husband while you were pregnant?"

"He was a very harsh person and always tried to suppress me. He possesses great abilities to hypnotize, it is known to the family that his grandfather was a magician."

"Any activity on the energy field level has to be strictly controlled, ethically" - I explained to the young man's mother. "If this is not the case then a increase in abilities blocks spiritual development, and this is what happened to your son. It's as if a car was picking up speed, but the driver started falling asleep. What kind of outcome would you expect from this ride, apart from an accident? High abilities and inner selfishness, received from his father, were supported by your resentment and hatred - as a result, a recoding of the energy field happened within your son, he turned into an instrument of destruction. If in earlier years, retribution would find this person only in his next life, today this process is shortened to just a few years.

A while ago when I was still working using the energy in my hands and couldn't see the cause for a disease, I tried to heal a three month old girl with an infection that wouldn't give in to antibiotics. I lit up a candle in the church for her health, and a few minutes later (as I figured out later) the girl fell into a coma and was taken to intensive care. That was another case of negative coding of a child's energy field. The girl's mother would often notice that if she got really upset with somebody it could lead to the offender's death. Focusing on hatred and resentment caused the recoding of the girl's energy field, and when the program of destruction clashed with the church's energy the girl almost died. This is similar to your son's situation."

"Very carefully review your whole life," – I continued. "recall all occasions where you experienced resentment and hatred, especially during your pregnancy. Mentally approach God and ask him for forgiveness, and then forgive everybody who offended you. Also mentally ask for forgiveness from everybody you could have offended in your life. Your husband should to do the same."

In two days the young man's parents told me that their son's mood started to improve, so now they had hope for his recovery.

I was convinced once again that the level of spirituality must always be higher than the level of a person's abilities.

Nowadays people have a very weak comprehension of what the subconscious is, therefore penetration into this, the most complicated and dangerous area, occurs not with high level of ethics, but at the quite primitive level of performance programs by "world class" psychics. The subconscious is too serious and dangerous an area, this is an area of the highest ethics, because on the energy field level we are all united and any violation automatically turns against the perpetrator. A lack of attention to ethical questions is dangerous because some people who are searching for knowledge can find themselves in contact with programs of self-destruction.

I examined the impact of scorcerers. How do they work? It turned out that if a scorcerer wants to harm his victim, he has to remove the victim's protection first. The best human protection is unity with the Universe: when we are united with the Universe we are invulnerable. A person will be left without any protection if this connection is broken, and this is possible only using the person's violations against the highest laws.

How does is work? Suppose I have some karmic violations: my father or mother hated somebody or resented somebody - that means they refused the Universe, refused love. Now these tiny spots in my energy field information structure received some support, were enhanced, and if before they had very little impact on my behavior, now, after receiving my support, they have great power in determining my behavior. The more I start to violate laws and the further the separation that takes place, my connection with the Universe weakens even more... scorcerers enhance the negative and the Universe itself destroys the aggressive person. Programs of destruction can act very creatively, can incite different kinds of aggression towards others and towards oneself – they can stimulate aggressive behavior, can significantly activate negative programs which are present in the person's energy field.

When a person strives for unity, love, compliance with the highest laws, his rapid spiritual growth begins and his energy field structures start to harmonize. This becomes his protection, his immune system and health, his descendants' and relatives' happy future.

If a person is aggressive, selfish, malicious, then through such action he supports the program of destruction whose embryo "sits" somewhere in his energy field - this leads to further destruction of his spiritual qualities and degeneration. As the church states: if a person is not striving towards God, he strives towards the devil. Since our thoughts, feelings and deeds are all recorded in the information field and affect our behavior and fate, then everything that is directed against the laws of love and unity separates us from the Universe, provoking the development and strengthening of destructive programs. Therefore even a random act can influence our fate. The entire purpose of ethics is to avoid the accumulation of negative karma, which after reaching a certain limit becomes active and starts destroying us and our children.

One day, parents of a year and a half year old boy came to consult with me. This was a difficult case - the child had stopped developing. I searched for the cause and found that the root of the disease lay in the killing of love. The parents killed the love in each other a few years before their son was born and this demolition of spiritual structures, very powerful and precisely aimed, formed the program that lived autonomously in the child's energy field. The boy's energy field structures were deformed so much that the purpose of his life was the destruction of other humans, and his organism had blocked this with a difficult disease.

If modern medicine were to learn how to cure the body, and manage the removal of this disease on the physical level, then we could expect the full degeneration of humanity, as the amount of people who live to destroy others would grow sharply. I am not talking about refusing to undergo medical treatments, but it has to be done correctly, otherwise Nostradamus's prophecy might come true: "At the end of this millennium there will be devil-people, and the purpose of their lives will be the destruction of other people."

In St Petersburg, the number of children suffering mental disease in recent years has increased dramatically - the blocking system working through the disintegration of mind and body. However medicine without understanding the true causes for disease, in my opinion, will soon overcome physical problems, not knowing what evil force will be released. The worst is that even communication with such a child on the energy field level can be dangerous.

I started healing the child and felt that I was being attacked. A year and a half year old child who lay in his mother's hands attacked me subconsciously. I found the same deformations as the child's in my own energy field. The destructive program was multiplying rapidly. At first I didn't feel well physically, but later all of the symptoms disappeared. At the same time my subtle spiritual structures began to collapse. Trying to help this child, I had received his program of destruction, which started to wreck my energy field structures.

Psychics who heal and don't see what and how they heal, who do not know the diagnostics of the energy field structures, can receive programs of destruction and, in the end, if they do not possess the highest spirituality and continuous spiritual aspiration, they can degenerate very quickly. These days this process is **already** evident.

A "virus" of spiritual demolition forces people to improve, in fact, this "virus" performs the duty of a forest warden, whose responsibility it is to eliminate dying organisms.

When I see complete spiritual disintegration, high aggression in childrens energy field structures, I understand the role of baptizm in church from the energy point of view. Christening has always affected the energy field structures, because church energy is focused on the most important parameter – spirituality. That's why, when a child with negative coding in his energy field, with a powerful deformation in his energy field structures, is brought to church, its influence on spirituality could lead to the straightening of the subtle structure deformation. Sometimes it can happen at the expense of a worsening physical state – the child could get seriously ill after baptizm, but in the end it heals his spiritual structures, his fate, his future and his children's future.

Chapter 7

Conclusion

The fact that human spiritual life rests on "three pillars" was known even to our ancestors. The first "pillar" is the ten commitments laid out in the Bible, the second – overcoming the seven deadly sins and the third – the three virtues.

If we have some understanding of the first "pillar" then not everybody can list all seven deadly sins.

As you may know, the Bible says nothing about the "deadly sins", they appeared later in theologians texts. It started when the Greek monk-theologian Evagrius from Pontus made a list of eight worst human passions; they are (in descending order of severity): pride, vanity, spiritual sloth, anger, despondency, greed, lust and gluttony.

At the end of the VI century pope Gregory I the Great shortened the list to seven, considering that vanity is the same as pride, spiritual sloth is just a variety of despondency and he added a new sin – envy. Also the list was rearranged: pride, envy, anger, despondency, greed, gluttony and lust.

I was interested in analyzing whether the same vices are energetically meaningful today and the following sequence appeared (in order of increasing severity of violations): gluttony, lust, greed, envy, anger, pride and despondency.

The world is changing and humanity has greatly expanded the list of sins, and some of them are more destructive than those that were known to our forefathers. Let's take a look at them.

1. The most grievous sin today – is late term abortion on or after the fifth month.

In the mother's womb the child, in fact, goes through the cycle of the universe's development and contacts with different entities, with different worlds, with the Divine, and he dwells in the closest communion with them during the fifth month of pregnancy.

The woman's state during pregnancy determines a lot in the future person's fate, therefore the mother's behavior first of all has to be subject to the child's interests. This involves a number of requirements:

- A child's spirit and spiritual potential is formed between conception and six months, therefore the woman during this period has to be focused on Divine feelings – love, kindness, humility and mercy. Food should be only dairy and plant based, which doesn't prevent the development of the child's spirit, and during the first two months – the intake of food should be minimal. After six months of pregnancy meat and fish are allowed, and delicatessens are allowed only after seven months;
- it is necessary to remember that the most important month is the fifth month, when the child and God are united;
- during pregnancy, a woman should be calm and patient, she should not feel resentment or any other negative emotions, she should calmly accept the present, prevent regrets about the past and not rush towards the future.

Quite often women suffer from toxicosis, which is the result of incorrect thinking and world outlook. When a relative denies a future child or has a negative attitude towards the future mother this can cause very significant energy distortions.

I listed only the most important requirements, the non-observance of which could cause great harm to the health and fate of a child.

2. Especially significant distortions of the energy field structures can be initiated by thoughts and actions aimed at killing the divine feelings in oneself or another person, as well as the betrayal of love for the sake of material wealth.

3. Third place is taken by regrets about the past, present and future, the desire to speed events up or slow them down - those are violations related to aggression against time.

4. Violations related to the feeling of hatred and resentment, a rude attitude towards people was discussed quite a bit already - these violations occupy fourth place.

I had to make a phone call to Belgium. I called the international phone service and heard an irritated voice:

"There is no Belgium today!" – and the line was disconnected without explanation.

I called the same number again. This time a calm, friendly voice politely explained, that orders were not accepted, and the next call could only be made the next day at five o'clock in the morning. I said thank you. Later I checked the energy field of the first telephone operator: after our conversation it was all distorted, and in the near future she may have different troubles and diseases, because my energy field was balanced and her rudeness came back to her, destroying her energy field structure.

So how many of those "self inflicted tortures" do we commit every day?

5. Fairly strong field distortions arise while verbally abusing living and nonliving objects.

The main rule for spiritual hygiene and a normal existence for human biofield structures is the fullness of love, because love is the highest manifestation of unity and world harmony.

The condition for meaningful existence is constant spiritual growth, the basis of which consists of love towards the Universe (as a whole), as well as love to parents, children and oneself (as parts of the whole). The transition from whole to part and back must be continuous, pulsating - then it corresponds to a harmonious world, carrying the joy of life and health.

All that remains to recall is the third "pillar" – the three virtues. These are Faith, Hope and Love. *"And now these three remain: faith, hope, love, but love is the greatest of these".*

The mistakes listed above are common, but there is also a separate series of very important warnings for those who are attracted to the method of diagnostics of karma. Once again, I want to warn all enthusiasts: the method is complicated and extremely dangerous. It is possible to learn the method of pandemotoric writing, but complications come from the fact that technical use of it without a high level of spirituality, constant analysis of emerging situations and constant caution can lead to unpredictable consequences. The main point is that this method is dangerous not only for the unprepared healer, but even more so for the patient. There are a number of particularities and conditions that are necessary to observe, otherwise it can be harmful for those involved.

Negative and incorrect energy influence on living nature is dangerous due to quick negative responses, but on inanimate nature it is slow, invisible, and has much more damaging consequences. As an example I will share the story of a young man who, after learning about the method, decided: "I want to do that too!"

"... I started to diagnose using the 'Lazarev method'. Everything seemed nice and easy. I was doing pretty well and bravely entered my karma, 'correcting flaws' and 'getting rid of vices'. I liked it a lot. My perception of various sensations changed, I analyzed every little headache and small pricking in the back.

Something was pushing me forward, and I became more active. I decided to get rid of all sins at once and started to trace my ancestors' behavior year by year, setting a goal for myself to discover all their acts that affected me and created my karma. Perhaps it did have some effect, but unexpectedly my wife and son got involved. When I would receive punishment for my mistakes, they would suffer as well, especially my son whom I love very much. I couldn't understand why they were responsible for my sins. I was working as hard as I could. I cleaned, diagnosed, and cleaned again. My son got a little bit better, but I started to receive attacks from my wife. This was a new problem and I rushed to solve this new problem.

At that point Lazarev warned me that the method in incompetent hands can have a negative impact on the people around. I couldn't find anything better to do than to take offence. The result was amazing: half of my energy field was gone – the left side of my energy field simply disappeared, that means that active self-destruction had begun. The feeling was not one of the best. On top of that, the same thing was happening to my son. I was really scared. I worried about my wife, my son and eventually myself. I realized the end could come very easily, and not just for me, but also for my family and loved ones.

Lazarev helped me get out of this situation. I wish I had stopped at that point, but my ambitions were pushing me forward. 'To catch up and surpass' – this memorized childhood slogan was my guide at that time. I started working with inanimate nature: tried to find malfunctions in cards and boards, breakages in automobiles and so on. Every time the disintegration of my energy field would follow. For people not familiar with bio-energetics I explain that in these conditions, a heart attack within three or four months is the least one can expect. That was my practice of 'the Lazarev method'.

I worked almost every day, but it looked like violations of the highest laws by my ancestors were inexhaustible, yet I still wanted to move on. Completely unexpectedly faults in my diagnoses started appearing. The range of physical sensations was extensive: from the contraction of the head in the temple areas and needlelike sensations, suddenly appearing in random places, to the incomparable feeling that there is no energy field above the top of the head. However the most difficult for me was to see my children suffering, knowing that this was my fault and no 'ambulance' would help. God forbid, but you too may go through this should you begin to engage in extrasensory diagnostics of karma.

This would be a great place to stop my reminiscence."

The essence of the method is not an increase of technical skills, but the development of a worldview and ethics. It's most dangerous and unacceptable to have a consumer's attitude towards the method. The rhythm of the Universe cannot be disrupted. Every person, aspiring for the Divine, gets filled with the highest energies and upon returning to Earth can transform them into material wealth. However if the spiritual laws haven't been felt deeply, didn't become a world view and way of life, and the person rushes to materialize this energy the result will be an abortion, not childbirth. Heightened pragmatism tends towards spiritual and material infertility.

When I attempt to teach somebody the method, I emphasize this first of all. At the beginning the teaching process appeared to me a little bit simplistically. Unfortunately, only a few can master the method, if anybody at all can be taught it.

I will provide just one example of the unexpected difficulties that can appear at any moment. I diagnosed a woman and described the most important violations of her penultimate incarnation. I was describing the nature of the violations and suddenly felt that I couldn't get accurate information. I analyzed the situation and my degree of information processing fell to zero. That meant that similar violations were present in my karma and my subconscious mind distorted information. I had to make corrections to my own energy field before I could proceed with the diagnosis.

The thing that saves me is my ability to monitor the situation all the time and my failure turns into victory - in this case it provoked the next round of purification of my own karma.

I constantly monitor the quality of received information while the majority of healers don't even know about the necessity to do so.

A young psychic shared his story with me:

"I always ask whether I am allowed to work or not"

"And who answers you?"

"Probably, the Divine," – an inarticulate answer followed.

"Are you sure about that?"

The young man got confused.

"Do you know, when you receive pure information and when it is distorted?" - There was no reply. "Many people attempt to work on your level...The mechanism is quite simple. To receive pure information a person has to be opened to the Divine. With 'dirty' karma, 'holding' your vacation house in one hand and your car in another, there is no chance to rise to these high levels.

You can only heal and receive pure information when you are in the state of 'closed' karma."

What is karma? This is a mechanism of requital for daily deeds, therefore one can 'close' one's karma by freeing the soul and the body from the material. Every healer and medium have to go through periods of fasting and strict limitations, they have to eliminate their dependency on material goods. Saints and prophets were true healers.

The karma of humanity is so impure that it is much more difficult to "close" karma now than it was in previous times.

Because consciousness and the subconscious, trust and knowledge are joined in the method of dialectical karmic diagnosis, applying the method one has to think and think and think some more.

Protecting the author of the story mentioned above while he was attempting to use my method, balancing his energy field structures helped to prevent him from serious problems, but his behavior is quite typical of one-sided thinking.

I will be happy if a person, upon reading this book, realizing how distorted our perception of the world has become - figures out what he has to change in his life to prevent the accumulation of new problems. The most important thing these days is to, at the very least, stop before "the edge". Any person can block his karma through correct behavior and proper food, this is the first step towards what is necessary, because the evil we face every day is inside us.

I found a statement in Chinese philosophy, that every person has to feel as if he were a savior of the world. According to the soviet textbook on psychiatry an analogous statement would be considered as the first sign of paranoia. Today, observing energy field interactions, I can certainly affirm that every person aspiring for the Divine is actively contributing to the saving of the world and becomes a savior of the world.

We already discussed that all processes in the Universe are dual. Aspiration for the Divine, to the starting point, from where the Universe was born, has to be accomplished by enhancing spirituality and increasing unity on the energy field level, but this process is impossible without the escalation of differentiation.

Mass, space and time are indications of the material world, and accordingly, development of the material world has to be expressed as an increase in mass, increase in space and an increase in time. Since time is correlated with space, in other words, with lengthiness, then the primary processes in the Universe on the material level must come to the widening of the Universe, which is in fact taking place. Time is developing, therefore, space is developing as well.

So then, a condition for the development and preservation of any process and object is physical differentiation with a simultaneous increase in energy field unity.

Differentiation on the physical level, in other words an increase in consumption and connection of the body to its environment, is doomed to destroy itself without spiritual preconditions. Differentiation is a develop-

ment and satisfaction of the body's needs that can lead to destruction and death if it's not preconditioned by spiritual support and spiritual growth. Thus, modern civilization is the manifestation of the spiritual search, which previous generations underwent throughout previous centuries - this determines the relation between the material and the spiritual in the world.

If we would extend this principle to a particular case – search for ways and methods of treatment - then the possibility of spiritual influence should go along with medical achievements. One important point to be remembered, that modern medicine wouldn't exist if thousands of years of seeking in the area of the soul and spiritual influence didn't lie at its root. The achievements of modern medicine are the manifestations of this seeking. In recent decades, medicine came to the edge where accumulated spiritual potential is already exhausted, so it has to return, like a prodigal son, to its origin – it has to realize that without understanding and a search for the causes of disease, further development is impossible.

Today we should be talking about the conflation of spiritual influence and medicine, with the preservation of the achievements of both, not their opposition. Disease is a tool for spiritual development, but our imperfection doesn't allow us to know the spirit fully and influence the disease using only spiritual methods. Therefore, something that is beyond the control of our imperfect spirit should be taken care of by medicine. The desire of medicine to have early diagnosis and to prevent disease – this is the first step towards spirituality, because every disease starts at the level of information. There are more and more facts accumulated in the world confirming that spiritual impact is more radical than medical.

Humanity slowly, but surely is returning to the Father, to spirit, spirituality and culture, because this is its only chance for salvation.